# Railway Memories

# *Return to*

# YORK

## PETER ROSE

With additional photographs by Adrian Booth, Stephen Chapman, Brian Myland, Cecil Ord, Keith Preston, British Rail, Ernest Sanderson, Peter Sutch.

**BELLCODE BOOKS**

10 RIDGE BANK TODMORDEN

LANCASHIRE OL14 7BA

Copyright © Bellcode Books

ISBN 1 871233 04 6

Published by Bellcode Books.

Edited by Stephen Chapman.

Printed by The Amadeus Press Ltd., Huddersfield.

Typeset by Highlight Type Bureau Ltd., Shipley.

**ABOVE:** The B16 4-6-0s, built by the NER from 1920 to the design of Sir Vincent Raven - some later rebuilt by the LNER - were literally York's own. All 69 of the class were once allocated there and only in early 1963 did significant numbers migrate away when about half the survivors went to Hull Dairycoates to see out the class's last year or so, mainly working passenger and freight trains back to York. No.61463, one of the B16/3s rebuilt by Edward Thompson from 1944 and among the last of the class to be withdrawn in 1964, makes a dramatic start from Branches Yard with the 3.20pm goods to Hull on 23rd January, 1963.

**FRONT COVER:** A rare view of new but grimy A1 4-6-2 No.60127, as yet un-named and wearing experimental blue livery, starting a southbound express out of York station in 1949. Two years later, Loco Yard signal box(left) and the gantry of semaphore signals would be swept aside by modernisation. *(Ernest Sanderson/Colour-Rail)*

**FRONTISPIECE:** A number of locomotives have carried names associated with York but V2 2-6-2 No.60847 *St. Peter's School York AD627*, seen reversing out of the North engine shed on 8th June, 1963, is probably the best known.

**BACK COVER(TOP):** A delightful reminder of how the various liveries of the old companies' engines enriched the wide variety of locomotive types seen at York. Jubilee 4-6-0 No.5594 *Bhopal*, still wearing LMS red in 1949, comes under the imposing Holgate signal gantry with a Bristol express composed of former LMS stock. *(Ernest Sanderson/Colour-Rail)*

**BACK COVER(BOTTOM):** Resignalling and electrification in 1988/89 together with the reduction in freight traffic have consigned this relatively recent view to history. BR blue-liveried class 47 No.47213 rolls a southbound Speedlink freight past a busy Dringhouses marshalling yard on 23rd July, 1981. *(Stephen Chapman)*

# INTRODUCTION

Gateway to the North - no other description of the railway at York could be more appropriate.

It is at this ancient city where for the last 140 years rail arteries from the South West, the Midlands and the other side of the Pennines have fed into the main East Coast route from London to Scotland.

Passing beneath the huge iron Holgate bridge on approaching York station, it always seemed as if the traveller was at that point leaving the south behind, while rounding the curves north of the station, past the engine sheds, carriage sidings and freight yards, there was no doubt that the North Country beckoned.

Every day, thousands of passengers changed between main line expresses and local or semi-fast trains for such places as Scarborough, Leeds, Sheffield and Hull. Engines were exchanged at York too, on both express passenger trains and, behind the scenes in the freight yards, on long-distance goods trains. In the days before restaurant cars, expresses also stopped there so that passengers could grab a hasty meal in the refreshment rooms.

Observers were forever delighted by the rich variety of operations and locomotives. York was the one place where massive Beyer-Garratt goods engines from the East Midlands rubbed shoulders with the sleek A4 Pacifics, where Jubilees, Royal Scots and Patriots of the old LMS came face to face with engines from East Anglia, and where North Eastern goods types swapped loads with their counterparts from the Great Northern and Great Central.

In **Railway Memories No.5** we concentrate especially on the 1950s and 60s, the earliest time many of us can remember seeing this great act being played out.

But because York changed so dramatically with the modernisation and electrification of the late 1980s, we have also, for the first time in Railway Memories, devoted a chapter to more recent times and scenes which many readers will recall just as fondly as the great days of steam.

**The same locomotive in the same spot as on the front cover - only 13 years later on 6th April, 1962. Loco Yard box and the semaphore signals have gone but the roundhouses of York South motive power depot remain as A1 No.60127 *Wilson Worsdell* manoeuvres the stock of an incoming express.**

# SETTING THE SCENE

In the early 19th century a York draper called George Hudson wasn't content to go on cutting cloth. He had bigger ideas and with a legacy left by an uncle, he was ready to start fulfilling his ambitions by whatever means it took.

At the same time, the York business community was calling for better transport links with the outside world. They had heard that a new mode of transport, called the railway, was proving to be a great success.

Their first thought was a link with the Stockton and Darlington Railway but attention later turned to a connection with the Leeds and Selby Railway and then, with eyes on London, to the North Midland Railway which was being built between Leeds and Derby.

In 1835, during a public meeting at York's famous Guild Hall, the York and North Midland Railway company was formed with this latter purpose in mind. George Hudson was appointed its chairman and George Stephenson was to be its engineer.

Hudson, who became known as the Railway King, is reported as saying "Mek' all t'railways come t' York" and that is just about what happened over the next 20 years,

with the city developing into the great meeting of routes and important railway industry centre that it still is today.

The first section of the YNMR was opened on 29th May, 1839 and ran from a temporary station in Queen Street, just outside the city wall, to a junction with the Leeds and Selby at Milford. Two more sections were added and on 1st July, 1840 the line from York to the North Midland at Altofts, near Normanton, was completed. A connection from Castleford to the North Midland at Methley gave access to Leeds.

The Great North of England Railway, meanwhile, was forging south from Darlington, opening completely by 30th March, 1841.

Also, in January, 1841, the two companies jointly opened York's first station, a terminus situated just inside the city wall through which a great arch had to be cut for the tracks to pass.

It comprised a fine Georgian building housing the booking hall and parcels office on the ground floor plus offices and the YNMR boardroom(more recently occupied by the regional traffic control) on the first. On the opposite(west) side were buildings

Although superseded by the present station in 1877, the original York station was still used for stabling and cleaning coaching stock when viewed from the city wall on 9th May, 1962. At the top left is the loading bay for car carrier services(later Motorail) and on the right the YNMR goods station, known locally as the Sack Warehouse. The 1906 NER headquarters dominates the skyline. In 1966 all track was lifted, part of the station roof demolished along with the sack warehouse, and the Motorail terminal moved to the main station. Since 1968, the entire foreground has been occupied by the Hudson House office block.

containing refreshment rooms and other facilities while between them were covered arrival and departure platforms with tracks connected by turnplates.

The YNMR established coal depots and a goods warehouse near the station while the GNE set up staithes on the river bank where coal brought from the North East was transhipped to barges for onward delivery.

By 1844, York had direct services to the Midlands, London and Gateshead, just a short ferry ride from Newcastle and close to achieving a link with Scotland.

In July, 1845, the YNMR opened the Scarborough line from a junction with the GNE at York North(York Yard South since 1938), with the branch to the East Riding market town of Market Weighton following just over two years later.

By this time Hudson's unscrupulous business methods were finding him out and within a couple more years the man who had risen to become York's Lord Mayor and a Member of Parliament was ruined.

Railway development continued, however, and in 1848 the East and West Yorkshire Junction Railway(absorbed by the YNMR three years later) opened a branch from Poppleton Junction(later renamed Skelton Junction) to Knaresborough. It was soon extended to Starbeck where it met the Leeds and Thirsk Railway (later the Leeds Northern) and, in 1862, to Harrogate.

In 1852 the YNMR completed a relatively short but important branch from Burton Salmon, on its York-Altofts line, to Knottingley. This provided a connection via the Lancashire and Yorkshire Railway to the Great Northern Railway just north of Doncaster, forming the first through route from Kings Cross to Tyneside.

Two years later, the YNMR, the York, Newcastle and Berwick(into which the GNE had evolved) and the Leeds Northern, merged to form the North Eastern Railway. Destined to become a profitable, innovative and mighty company, it chose York as its headquarters, though the station offices, even with another floor added on top, were insufficient to accommodate all departments.

By this time York's basic railway structure was in place though more refinements followed. In 1865 the Market Weighton line was extended to Beverley, forming a through route to Hull as originally intended, and in 1869 the Church Fenton to Micklefield line was opened, giving a more direct route to Leeds. Two years later the direct route to Selby and Doncaster was completed, establishing the true East Coast main line and enabling London expresses to avoid the Knottingley detour.

On 1st January, 1880, the Foss Islands branch opened to serve the increasingly important York cattle market in the east of the city. Foss Islands also acted as a general goods station and several industrial concerns eventually had railway systems sprouting off the 1 mile 1,266-yard branch, the biggest being at Rowntree's chocolate factory.

Although goods only, the branch carried a regular passenger service for Rowntree's workers as far as a halt next to the factory until its withdrawal, after 61 years' operation, on 8th July, 1988. Occasional excursions also ran.

The final piece in the jigsaw was added in 1913 when the Derwent Valley Light Railway, an independant company formed by farmers and landowners along the fertile plain east of York, was opened to serve their agricultural needs. It ran 16 miles from Layerthorpe, alongside Foss Islands, to Cliff Common, on the Selby-Market Weighton line. Much freight traffic passed to and from the DVLR for nearly 70 years although its regular passenger service ceased in 1926.

As the railways into York grew busier and more important, the existing station proved to be a handicap. Trains between London and Scotland had to reverse there, Scarborough and Hull trains had to reverse at York North, and the station was generally inadequate for the traffic on offer.

Consequently, the NER built the present station, a magnificent structure dominated by an 800ft-long, 81ft-span arched roof reaching 42ft above platform level. This was flanked by 55ft-span arches over bay platforms on either side and extra 43ft-span arches on the east side, one each to the north and south of the station buildings.

Completed in June, 1877, it was situated on a new line from Queen Street to Poppleton Junction which removed the need for trains to reverse. The Scarborough lines from York North remained for goods traffic, being crossed on the level by the new route.

Numerous depots, workshops and engine sheds grew up in York and at an early stage the YNMR founded an engine shed and locomotive works in Queen Street. It grew to

It has been said that of all York's historical buildings, only the Minster and the 1877 station are of great architectural merit. This view looking south from platform 8 North on 16th September, 1958, shows the magnificent arched roof and the sweeping curves of the platforms to good effect. *(by courtesy of British Rail)*

include two large erecting shops, a boiler shop and machine shops but produced few new locomotives, being limited mainly to major repairs and rebuilds.

The works closed in 1905, its operations switched to Darlington, and within four years the boiler shop was converted to an engine shed for the Lancashire and Yorkshire Railway. One of the erecting shops was eventually turned into a Railway Institute gymnasium, and one of the machine shops into the original York railway museum. Another workshop became the Road Motor Engineer's garage where railway road vehicles were maintained.

In 1841 the GNER established a straight engine shed between Queen Street and York North Junction, other sheds being added soon after and together with roundhouses built by the NER in the 1850s and 60s, they formed the York South motive power depot.

When the huge York North shed, consisting of three roundhouses under one roof, opened in 1877, many NER locomotives were transferred there from the South shed and the resulting spare accommodation was let to other companies.

One of the original engine sheds was demolished so that the present station could be built, another went in the 1930s to make room for station extensions, while one of the roundhouses was destroyed by fire in 1921. Remarkably, the first GNE shed and the other two roundhouses survived until the end of 1963.

A wagon works founded near North Junction in 1867 replaced workshops previously housed in the Queen Street complex, while the carriage works, which grew to huge proportions, was set up on the other side of the GNE line in 1884.

It built and repaired coaches for the whole of the NER and since the 1950s has been assocated especially with the construction of new electric multiple units for the Southern Region and London commuter routes and, since the 1980s, diesel units as well.

In 1906, the NER opened its new headquarters building to overcome the ongoing shortage of office accommodation. Overlooking the old station, it was as palatial inside as it was magnificent on the outside.

The York offices became the headquarters of the North Eastern area of the London and North Eastern Railway into which the NER and its partners on the East Coast were grouped in 1923, and upon nationalisation in 1948, the headquarters of the North Eastern Region of British Railways. From 1st January, 1967 the Eastern and North Eastern Regions were merged and York became the new Eastern Region's headquarters. To accommodate the migration of staff from the old ER headquarters in London, a new office block was built between the city wall and the old station to house the technical departments. Called Hudson House in honour of the Railway King, it opened in 1968.

Up to the second world war, changes on

the ground largely reflected an expanding industry and included the addition of the island platforms 15 and 16.

Changes of another sort were made on the night of 29th April, 1942 when the war and the German Luftwaffe came to York. Two high explosive bombs and a hail of incendiaries reduced the roof over platforms 1-3 to a mass of tangled metal, platform 9 was blocked by the burnt out remains of the 10.15pm Kings Cross to Edinburgh, the station master's, booking and parcels offices were destroyed and the refreshment rooms badly damaged. A direct hit on the North shed turned B16 4-6-0 No.925 and A4 Pacific No.4469 *Sir Ralph Wedgewood* into scrap metal. The damage and casualties would have been far worse but for the bravery of rail staff who, with help from the military, had the burnt and battered station back in full operation the following evening.

Then, in 1951, the most advanced and biggest route relay interlocking signalling system in the world was completed. Some of the world's most impressive mechanical signal boxes gave way to just one control centre situated in the station, while the towering gantries of wooden slotted signals that had stood guard over the station approaches for many decades were replaced by neat and efficient colour lights.

Always a fascinating place to observe railway operations, York was the point where the most famous expresses and locomotives on their way between the English and Scottish capitals met with intrepid cross-country trains from places like Bristol, Bournemouth, Liverpool and Lowestoft, as well as secondary services from Scarborough, Leeds, Sheffield and Hull.

As a result, the station saw a great variety of locomotives well into the 1960s, the Jubilees, Royal Scots and Patriots of LMS pedigree standing side by side with the LNER's thoroughbred Pacifics, while fussy J71 and J72 tanks moved coaches, refreshment cars and parcels vans between platforms and sidings. The goods yards and engine sheds routinely saw ex-Great Central and Great Northern 2-8-0s alongside ex-LMS Beyer-Garratts, WD and 8F 2-8-0s.

York was also an important centre for the remarshalling, staging, and changing of engines and crews on the heavy long-distance freight trains which day and night snaked their way between Holgate Junction and York Yards. There were Up and Down hump yards in this area, along with groups of sidings at Skelton Yard, Skelton New Yard(built with government money in 1941 for the war effort) and Dringhouses. The marshalling yards dealt with traffic connecting into and out of trunk services while the trips which serviced local depots and stations mainly used Branches Yard, situated alongside the station.

Originating and incoming traffic largely reflected York's position in a major agricultural area. It was one of the biggest centres in the North East for livestock until BR began to pull out of such business in the late 1960s and had cattle docks at Holgate as well as Foss Islands. Incoming traffic included coal for city depots in Leeman Road, Foss Islands and at Layerthorpe where from 1964 the DVLR's mechanised facilities could handle 40,000 tons a year. Coal was also delivered via the Foss Islands branch to Rowntree's chocolate factory, the city gas works, power station, and the

The 1841 Great North of England engine shed was used by the Great Northern Railway until after formation of the LNER when GN section engines moved to the North shed. In 1933, the LMS took over and the shed survived, somewhat modified, until November, 1963.

It still had its original hipped roof in the early 1930s when hosting LNER A1 Pacific (later A3) No.4480 *Enterprise*. (Cecil Ord)

railway's own laundry. There was also petrol(ESSO and BP), domestic heating oil for Layerthorpe, sand from Norfolk and soda ash from Cheshire to Foss Islands for a nearby glass works, seed potatoes, and military traffic for barracks in the area.

Originating freight once included flour and animal feeds from the large Leetham's Mill, Foss Islands, enough confectionary from Rowntrees to make up two trains a day even in the 1980s and substantial tonnages of grain from the DVLR to Scotland.

In the season, sugar beet was brought from surrounding farms to the British Sugar Corporation factory in Poppleton Road where two Barclay 0-4-0STs, later replaced by a Ruston diesel, also marshalled wagons of pulp and mollasses for despatch elsewhere.

General merchandise and sundries were handled at the main goods depot in Leeman Road until 1972 when some of the last rail traffic was clothes for Marks and Spencer distributed under the Fashionflow banner. All BR freight was then concentrated on Foss Islands and the warehouse ultimately became part of the National Railway Museum.

Today, no freight whatsoever enters or leaves York by rail, the traffic either having been lost to road or disappeared with the industry it served.

All kinds of railway support activities grew up in York, such as depots and workshops for civil, signal and outdoor machinery engineers. There were even two railway gas works - one near York Yard North(originally known as Gas Works Junction) which produced gas from coal, and another next to the engine shed on Leeman Road for making gas from oil. The laundry dealt with linen from railway hotels, while a small printing works in the hotel grounds produced restaurant and dining car menus until the early 1980s. The LNER opened a garage, later known as Foxton's Garage, on Leeman Road for the benefit of hotel guests, while in nearby Poppleton there was, and still is, a nursery which produces flowers for stations and prepares floral displays for special occasions.

York got off relatively lightly from the ravages of the 1960s Beeching era in which lines and stations seemed to close daily. The service to Pickering via Pilmoor had gone in 1953, but the only actual railway out of the city to close was the Beverley line which went in November, 1965, while through trains to Whitby were withdrawn on 8th March.

The former Queen Street boiler shop was used as an engine shed until 1933 when the LMS moved to the old GNE shed. It was then used for storing museum exhibits, stabling locomotives and, in the late 1950s, as a temporary diesel depot for York's first diesel shunters. During the early 1960s a Pacific or V2, such as 60848 on 23rd May, 1962, could be seen there on standby in case one of the insurgent diesels broke down.

The shed was also used for storing officers' saloons until 1968 when the roof fell in, destroying one saloon. It was later demolished and the site is now a car park.

Until 1987, York was a point where cross-country or Trans-Pennine expresses changed engines, an activity which greatly enhanced the variety of operations there. On 2nd April, 1962, York A1 No.60140 *Balmoral* prepares to hand over the 12.43 Newcastle-Bristol to Jubilee 4-6-0 No.45564 *New South Wales* at the south end of platform 14.

However, the end of steam and the run-down of local freight traffic saw a big reduction in facilities for such operations. Closure of Branches Yard was one example, although the new hump yard opened at Dringhouses in 1961 for dealing exclusively with modern fully braked express freight trains, was getting steadily busier.

The North steam shed became the National Railway Museum which in 1983 also took over the adjacent repair depot following the end of all main line locomotive maintenance in York.

Also in 1983, the 1871 Selby line was replaced by a new high-speed route taking East Coast expresses around the Selby coalfield and the mining subsidence which would otherwise have slowed them to a crawl.

Other changes in the 1980s included the complete closure of the Derwent Valley Railway, the end of all local freight traffic, closure of the Foss Islands branch and Dringhouses marshalling yard, the modernisation and closure of Clifton carriage depot, and privatisation of the carriage works.

In 1984 the government gave British Rail the go-ahead to electrify the East Coast main line, heralding sweeping modern-isation that would alter York's railway beyond recognition.

Before the overhead wires to power the new InterCity 225 trains were put up, the complex track layout, little changed since the 1930s, was substantially slimmed down while signalling was brought under the country's most sophisticated solid state interlocking system covering 42 route miles.

To operate it, an electronic control centre was built on the site of the fruit dock sidings, between the station and the Scarborough goods lines, the remains of which were also abandoned. The through lines between platforms 8 and 9 were taken up, as was the track into platforms 2, 4, 5, 6, and 12. One new piece of track was a triangle on the site of the South shed, installed primarily for turning track maintenance machines. The platforms were also renumbered - Nos.3, 7, 8, 9, 10, 11, 13, 14, 15, 16 becoming 1, 2, 3 (the Scarborough end became platform 4), 5, 6, 7, 8, 9, 10 and 11 respectively.

After an uncertain spell, York now looks like continuing as an important railway centre. The station remains a major interchange for passengers and mails while freight trains are still staged and re-manned in York and Skelton yards. Late in 1993, the carriage works, threatened with closure due to a lack of work, won a major order to build new electric trains for the London commuter network, while two zones of Railtrack, the authority which took over British Rail's infrastructure in April, 1994 as part of the railway privatisation process, and two train operating companies, have their headquarters at York.

Electrification, completed in 1991, established the East Coast main line as the country's premier InterCity route. By 1996, thanks to the Channel Tunnel, York passengers will be able to travel by futuristic Eurostar express direct to Paris and Brussels while international freight trains may well be passing through York Yards within weeks of this book being published.

# THIS WAS YORK

It was at York in the early 1960s that Bellcode Books publisher Stephen Chapman endulged his newly-acquired obsession for railways.

"My earliest memories of railways in York were not of the famous station but on the riverside in the city centre. A break at the cafe in Leak and Thorpe's department store during Saturday shopping trips in the 1950s was a special treat - not so much for the buns but the spectacular view across the river to Blundy and Clark's coal depot on the opposite bank. Here, on a short stretch of track were a couple of steam-powered grabs used for lifting coal out of barges and how I enjoyed watching them bustling up and down amid clouds of steam. As I recall, the activity continued into the early 1960s when the depot closed to be replaced by the Viking Hotel.

"The first I remember of York station was in August, 1959 during a journey with my mother from Cambridge to Hull. For the first time, I was noting the numbers of engines I saw on the way but my only recollection of York was of an engine slipping violently - as they often did - while trying to heave its northbound express out of platform 9. Its volcanic exhaust erupted with an ear-splitting roar high into the roof girders, bringing down spots of wet soot and driving the pigeons into panic. The number I wrote down was 6000 but I doubt if it was Great Western 4-6-0 *King George V* and I had clearly missed a digit - 60500 or 60800 perhaps.

"I was older and wiser the next time I visited York station. That was on a Sunday in spring, 1961 during a journey to Scarborough.

"I was only there for a short time but what I saw was enough to hook me for good.

"My parents receded into the buffet while this 10 year-old peered longingly through the railings that divided the concourse from the adventureland of 16 bustling platforms.

"First in my notebook was A4 No.60021 *Wild Swan* on a London express - a good start but the next engine I saw backing through the station was better still. It was Carlisle A3 No.60093 *Coronach* and the first of that illustrious class that I had seen.

"Even then, there was a more exciting engine which I could plainly see beyond the far end of the footbridge in platform 15 - grimy and unsung ex-Great Northern J6 0-6-0 No.64191. My school friends never believed it.

"More believable but no less exciting was the engine heading our train to Scarborough - first B1 No.61000 *Springbok*.

"My next visit - on 8th August - was another mind-blowing experience. For an 11th birthday treat, my mother took myself and a friend to the engine sheds in Leeman Road!

"What we saw as we wandered down North Eastern Crescent, a row of railway cottages leading from Leeman Road to the shed yard - left us speachless.

"Before us stood rows on rows of smoking iron monsters. Many were of types I had only ever seen in books - Great Central 2-8-0s, a variety of ex-LMS types, and BR Standards, including Nos.70000 *Britannia*, 70003 *Geoffrey Chaucer* and 70037 *Hereward the Wake*.

"After the shed visit my mother went shopping and left the pair of us on the station for a couple of hours before taking us to the railway museum in Queen Street.

"On our way into the station we saw a green tank engine in the sidings leading into the old station. This we had never heard of before but we soon learned that it was celebrated J72 0-6-0T No.68736 in its North Eastern Railway colours.

"We planted ourselves with all the other spotters on platform 9 North where there was a huge wooden bench - but you had to be there early to get a seat.

"Our day's observation produced eleven East Coast Pacifics, among them five `Streaks' which included the splendid sight of 60012 *Commonwealth of Australia* seen from our approaching train as it waited to enter the station with an express from the north. A superb day was rounded off with a cavalcade of J27 0-6-0s, J94 0-6-0STs and original B16s making their way from the yards to the shed.

"Subsequent visits to this grand station were not just about engines, though. There were plenty of other attractions, such as the

The bench at the north end of platform 9 was usually packed with spotters, but on 8th August, 1962 uncharacteristic rain had driven all but the hardiest souls under the cover of the station roof to watch the departure of A3 Pacific No.60103 *Flying Scotsman*.

old printer for stamping your name on metal luggage tags - only we stamped out loco names - and the Stephenson's Rocket in a glass case whose wheels turned for a penny in the slot.

"A box of sandwiches - not marmite but egg, usually, and a bottle of cherryaid provided the all-important sustenance. So did the platform 14 buffet's wonderful asparagus soup which I sipped while watching comings and goings in platforms 14-16 and the sidings beyond.

"Saturday visits to York became a regular thing during 1962 when the first job after getting off the train was always to check the station before going off to `bunk' the shed. Sometimes we were greeted by the roar of a Kylchap blastpipe behind the arched wall hiding platforms 14-16, but on 17th July the roar was stronger than usual. Investigation revealed the marvellous spectacle of A4s 60013 *Dominion of New Zealand* and 60015 *Quicksilver* standing side by side after arriving with Race Day specials.

"Reaching the shed, we always started by peeping through the open windows of the repair shop where we once saw an unidentifiable industrial 0-4-0ST and on another occasion, pioneer A4 60014 *Silver Link*.

"From there we slipped behind the derelict oil gas works to a little door which led into the main roundhouse. Passing gingerly through this door was like entering another world. The darkness and the heavy, brooding atmosphere made you feel as though you were going into the trogdolite dwelling of some huge beast. In reality the beasts were A1 and A2 Pacifics ranged around the two turntables like thoroughbred racehorses in a stable. They were flanked by V2s, B1s and B16s, K1s, J27s and Ivatt 2-6-0s.

"Entry was of course strictly illicit - notices warned of a 40 shilling fine - but no-one seemed mind.

"In the summers of 1963 and 64 I excelled, spending a full week each year at the station, courtesy of an aunt in Acomb who fed me and gave me a bed for each night. I am eternally grateful to her.

"Those weeks, especially the one in 1963, were magic. York always managed above all to delight with an incredible variety of engine types and with so many changes taking place that year as a result of advancing dieselisation and shed closures, there seemed to be even more classes than ever.

"My first day, 17th August, opened with the splendid sight of spotless A1 No.60114 *W.P.Allen* heading confidently past the shed with a northbound express but what stick in my mind most are the Britannias that were still reaching York from March and Immingham. During that week, I saw Nos.70008 *Black Prince* and 70035 *Rudyard Kipling* (on the 17th), 70006 *Robert Burns*, 70007 *Coeur-de-Lion* and 70011 *Hotspur* (on the 19th), 70006 and 70007 (on the 20th) and 70006 again on the 21st.

"I also saw a total of four different A4s, eleven A3s, eleven A1s, 29 V2 2-6-2s, 24 B1 4-6-0s, six B16 4-6-0s, 18 K1 2-6-0s, two O1 2-8-0s, nine O4 2-8-0s, O2 2-8-0 No.63961, two J27 0-6-0s, two `Crab' 2-6-0s, Stanier 2-6-0 No.42952, five Ivatt 4MT 2-6-0s, 18 Black Five 4-6-0s, seven Jubilee 4-6-0s, Royal Scot 4-6-0 No.46133 *The Green Howards*, three 8F 2-8-0s, three BR Standard 3MT 2-6-0s, Standard 2MT 2-6-0 No.78010, three BR Standard 3MT 2-6-2Ts, 20 9F 2-10-0s, and no less than 42 WD 2-8-0s.

"Scarborough and Malton sheds closed in April,1963 and of their surviving engines, Ivatt 2-6-2Ts 41251/65, Standards 82026-9 and J27s Nos.65844/49/88 were present at York that summer. Most were initially consigned straight to storage in the South shed but 41265 and 65849 were already withdrawn. The Standards were sent on to the Southern Region, 41251 was transferred to Lancaster after only a short spell at York, while 65888 put in a few months at York before being withdrawn. Only 65844 saw any great length of active service there, lasting until the end of 1965.

"Also going into the South Shed was Stanier Class 3 2-6-2T No.40117. It had been withdrawn for several months, yet even after the South shed was demolished it was still to be found, looking well cared for, in the North shed well into 1964.

"The south shed always attracted me, as if it held some great secret waiting to be discovered. One Saturday afternoon in 1962 when all was quiet a companion and myself slipped across the foot crossing off the end of platform 16 and into the collection of brooding old buildings. We peered expectantly through the broken windows of the small roundhouse but its black, empty interior revealed only the old 42ft turntable and the 16 rusty tracks radiating from it. We moved on to the large, roofless roundhouse but again found only a disused 45ft

The mystery of what lay behind the south shed, out of view from the station platforms, was always a strong lure to the more adventurous. On 1st August, 1962, however, nothing more exciting than York WD 2-8-0s Nos.90424 and 90571 was stored at the north end of the ex-GNE straight shed. The roofless shell of the larger roundhouse, once used by the Midland Railway, is on the right.

Leisurely observation on endless sunny summer Saturdays was how it seemed to be on the platform ends at York in the early 1960s. At the south end of platform 8 on 8th September, 1962, B1 4-6-0 No.61337 was about to uncouple from its terminating train on a day that diversions were in force due to a blockage on the London main line. A York stalwart, 61337 was still active there on the day the North shed closed to steam in June, 1967.

turntable, the 18 stalls leading from it partially obscured by colourful shafts of willow herb. There were, alas, no secrets and the only engines were those we already knew of in the straight shed.

"The last time I saw the South sheds was late on an autumn afternoon in 1963, their gaunt outlines, especially the gables and chimney stacks of the large shed, looking eerily beautiful against the red sky of a particularly vivid sunset. The next time I went to York, there was only an empty space.

"The year 1964 was the first in which I noticed a really serious decline in steam and my summer stay was as full of forboding as it was excitement.

"The last of the historic B16s - a part of the York scene which I had taken for granted - were withdrawn a few weeks earlier, having seen out their final months working from Hull. The A4s, source of so much excitement over the years, had departed for exile in Scotland and would hardly ever be seen in York again in normal service.

"There was still plenty of interest, though. York had a big allocation of A1s while A3s came in from New England, Gateshead and Darlington. Possibly the high spot of my 1964 week was the sight of 60045 *Lemberg* on a southbound troop train from Catterick.

"But the rundown was on. By 1965, many A1s and V2s were in store although over the last few years York had enjoyed a considerable influx of the Pacifics with old favourites like *Silurian* and *Boswell* being joined by such newcomers as *Holyrood*, *Great Central* and *Borderer*.

"There were still a few steam passenger workings in summer, 1965 and it was on one, the 15.40 Saturdays Only to Hull via Market Weighton, that I made my rather premature last run with BR steam. The engine was B1 No.61256 and I went home early so that I could ride with it to Pocklington rather than with the usual English Electric Type 4 on the 17.40.

"Come 1966, with steam now fading, my local railway closed and my interests turning elsewhere, I struggled to summon up the enthusiasm for a trip to York. Late one grey, dismal October afternoon, I made the effort and went after school. I found many steam locos either on the scrap line or stood without work. The atmosphere was so depressing that I didn't want to bother anymore.

"On 6th February, 1967 I was back but this time starting my working life as a probationary clerk in British Rail's Eastern Region permanent way section, situated in what used to be the booking hall of the original station. The railway was not an automatic career choice but offered better conditions. As a school leaver I had two jobs to choose from - something else that has changed a lot since.

"Lunch among the enginemen and shed staff in Leeman Road canteen gave me the opportunity to revisit the shed, but there was little to see. The diesels now held sway and the only engine I saw in steam during lunchtime was a solitary Hull B1 being serviced between turns. I can still see a rather rundown looking 61010 *Wildebeeste* simmering at the north end of the yard, the steam from its safety valves and several other places flitting away in the chill wind. The only other active steam loco I might see was a K1 in the distant p-way yard.

"That wasn't the only steam at York by then, of course, and if I caught the early bus to work I would be just in time to see York's last regular steam passenger working depart for Manchester via Wakefield, usually in the hands of a Normanton Black Five or Fairburn 2-6-4T.

"York shed closed to steam in June, 1967 and at least I was there to record the end which saw B1s Nos.61030/35, 61319 and 61337, and Standard 2-6-0 No.77012 in steam ready for transfer elsewhere. Stood alongside them were their replacements - brand new Class 20s in the D8300 series and Class 47s in the D1100 series.

"There were many sad sights to be seen at York shed over the next months with engines on their way from the North East to scrapyards further south but none were sadder than the wreck of Class 50 prototype diesel No.DP2, sheeted over after being destroyed in the terrible collision with the derailed Cliffe-Uddingston cement train near Thirsk on 31st July.

"During that summer, my horizons were broadened when I was loaned to other sections of our department, namely the concrete depot and soil mechanics laboratory in Leeman Road.

"From my greenhouse-style office, I could watch the Class 03 diesels shunting the goods depot and, alas, see the bulk of the wagon works being demolished.

"The concrete depot itself manufactured all kinds of concrete items from fence posts to signal cable troughs and, as I recall, we sent an awful lot to the Southern Region. Among the things we did not make were sleepers and large structural items. Most of the output left by rail then, often in shock-absorbing open wagons.

"In 1969 I was given the job of programming work for the Eastern Region's Neptune track recorders - self-propelled trolleys just smaller than a small diesel shunter - which recorded the condition of the track on both a graph and a computer print-out which were then used by the technical staff to plan the regular maintenance programme.

"We had two machines - No.1(later replaced by No.13) for the old North Eastern area and No.9 for the old Eastern Region. All of British Rail's Neptune machines were repaired at the Regional Plant Workshops at the far end of Leeman Road. This meant that non-recording movements were made from all over the country to York and back, the Eastern Region portions of which I arranged with the operating department.

"I continued this work until 1973, by which time the prototype HST was breaking speed records during trials north of York and the railway I first knew was going for good."

The final day of steam at York shed was 25th June, 1967, when the last workable engines were lined up awaiting transfer to a few more months' activity elsewhere. In steam with BR Standard Class 3 2-6-0 No.77012 were B1 4-6-0s Nos. 61337(left), 61030 *Nyala* (right) and 61035 *Pronghorn*. (Stephen Chapman)

# SOUTH TO NORTH THROUGH YORK

Bolton Percy station, seven and a half miles south of York, was served by trains using the YNMR Normanton lines until its closure on 13th September, 1965. The signal box lasted somewhat longer while the goods yard on the left of the above picture was closed by 27th April, 1964. In summer, 1957, Bolton Percy was served by three weekday trains to Leeds, two to Normanton, two to Sheffield, five to York and, on Saturdays, one to Blackpool.

This sequence shows B1 No.61353 rolling a northbound express goods along the Down Normanton line and(left) past the signal box and lofty NER slotted signals on 22nd March, 1963. The fireman with his metal-stemmed pipe was familiar figure in the York area.

Top: Racing the 9.38am York-Manchester parcels through Bolton Percy along the Up Leeds line on 23rd March, 1963 is Black Five 4-6-0 No.44823.

Left: The ex-NER D20 4-4-0s were regular performers around York until their demise in the 1950s. One of the last survivors, No.62387, approaches Copmanthorpe on the Down Leeds line with a Railway Correspondence and Travel Society railtour on 23rd June, 1957. *(Ernest Sanderson)*

Bottom: Copmanthorpe Moor level crossing as it was in the 1930s with individual sets of gates for the Leeds and Normanton lines and an LNER K3 2-6-0 heading light along the Down Normanton. The crossing was later equipped with barriers but closed altogether on opening of the East Coast main line Selby diversion in 1983 which saw numerous high speed trains routed through the village. *(Ernest Sanderson)*

# SHORT MEMORIES

**29th July, 1957:** Hull-based diesel multiple units take over most York-Hull via Market Weighton services, becoming the first DMUs to regularly reach York and rendering a number of D49 4-4-0s redundant.

**August, 1957:** York-based BR Standard Class 5 4-6-0 73170 regularly hauls the Yorkshire Pullman between Harrogate and Leeds after working 7.15am York-Harrogate.

**October, 1957:** Lincoln-based experimental diesel electric multiple unit converted from London Midland loco-hauled coaches 9821/8 and fitted with 450hp underfloor Davey Paxman engines reaches York during a test run.

Above: Copmanthorpe station closed to passengers on 5th January, 1959 but it was still intact when Black Five No.44782 was passing along the Up Normanton line with the 9.38am York to Manchester parcels on 20th March, 1963. The loading dock of the goods yard(closed 4th May, 1964) was the photographer's vantage point.

Below: The bridge carrying Station Road over the railway was the vantage point for this shot of WD 2-8-0 No.90417 trundling a northbound coal train through the station on the same day.

When open, Copmanthorpe had a rather spartan service, being served in summer, 1957 by just three weekday trains to York, three to Leeds and one each to Sheffield and Normanton.

Left: In this pre-war view, ex-Great Central 0-6-0 No.5293 heads an express goods along the Up Normanton line towards Copmanthorpe.

Centre: The huge 2-6-6-2 Beyer-Garratts of the LMS frequently reached York with coal and iron ore trains from the East Midlands until being replaced by 9F 2-10-0s in the 1950s. No.47992 was still in LMS livery when approaching Chaloner's Whin Junction in 1949. *(both Ernest Sanderson)*

Below: The East Coast and Leeds/ Normanton lines parted company at Chaloner's Whin Junction, 2 miles south of York station, until 1983 when the Selby diversion opened and Chaloner's Whin was replaced by a new junction at Colton, just south of Copmanthorpe. This was Chaloner's Whin on 15th March, 1961 with 9F 2-10-0 No.92193 taking an empty stock train onto the Up Normanton line.

**Right: A BR 204hp 0-6-0 diesel shunter (class 03) leaves the former Naburn station behind as it ambles along the East Coast main line towards Selby. Naburn station closed on 8th June, 1953 and the goods yard(left), its four sidings, loading dock and coal drops, on 6th July, 1964.**
*(E. Sanderson)*

**Above: The York-Selby line crossed the River Ouse by the swing bridge at Naburn which was once topped by its own signal box. On 23rd May, 1961 K3 2-6-0 No.61812(with GNR tender) was photographed from the box while approaching the bridge with a southbound tank train.**

**Right: Another railway at Naburn was the 2ft gauge system at the City of York sewerage works where the two 1937-built Ruston 4-wheel diesels were rusting out of use by December, 1975.** *(Stephen Chapman)*

Above: In 1935, the first of the LNER's famous streamlined expresses, the Silver Jubilee, was introduced along with the magnificent A4 Pacifics. For working this prestige express, the first batch of A4s were finished in silver grey livery, such as No.2511 *Silver King*, seen gathering speed with the London-bound train while rounding the curve from Chaloner's Whin and passing under the A64 Tadcaster Road. *(Cecil Ord)*

Below: In another vintage scene, a former Lancashire and Yorkshire Hughes 4-6-0 has a good head of steam as it passes Dringhouses signal box(opened for first world war traffic) with a pre-Second World War express to Manchester Victoria via Wakefield Kirkgate. This service was withdrawn in 1970. *(Ernest Sanderson collection)*

# SHORT MEMORIES

**7.12.58:** Clan Pacific 72003 *Clan Fraser* and Black Five 45316 arrive at Dringhouses with special freights from Garston, Merseyside. Both turn at York shed before returning light to Mirfield.

**5.1.59:** Diesel multiple units begin operating an enhanced York-Sheffield local service.

**4.7.59**: V3 2-6-2T 67684 makes a rare appearance in York with the 12.8pm from Hull.

**11.7.59:** 4F 0-6-0 44184 works through York on the 11.35am Scarborough -Derby and D49/2 4-4-0 62762 *The Fernie* arrives with the 12.38pm from Scarborough.

Dringhouses marshalling yard was established in 1915 to deal with extra goods traffic created by the first world war. In 1961, it was totally rebuilt as an automated hump yard, the first in the country for dealing exclusively with fully-braked express freight trains. The yard closed in 1987 when its remaining work was switched to Doncaster.

Above: With the Dringhouses hump and control tower on the right, Mirfield-based B16/3 No.61461, heads south with a permanent way train, a typical Monday morning working, on 29th October, 1962.

Below: A brace of B16s, B16/2 No.61435 and B16/3 No.61464, move a long evening express goods out of the yard and head for the south on 8th August, 1962.

# SHORT MEMORIES

**28.7.59:** Preserved LSWR 4-4-0 563, SECR 4-4-0 737 and LBSCR 0-6-0T *Boxhill* pass through York while being moved from store at Tweed-mouth to Eastleigh and, in the case of 737, to Ashford.

**2.7.60:** Bristol-based Jubilee 45651 *Shovell* works out of York on the 8.14am to Hull via Market Weighton.

**16.7.60:** Sulzer type 2s D5096 and D5098 double-head the 8.23am Newcastle-Lowestoft and 9am Ely-Newcastle between York and Newcastle.

**23.7.60:** Britannia 70013 *Oliver Cromwell* hauls the 8.35am Newcastle-Bournemouth West out of York.

Above: A 350hp 0-6-0 diesel shunter occupies the Dringhouses hump as 9F 2-10-0 No.92149 passes with a southbound block steel train on 24th March, 1962. During 1962, its first full year of operation, Dringhouses yard marshalled approximately 850 wagons a night into 30 trains bound for the south, the west and the Midlands.
Below: The Newcastle-Manchester Red Bank empty news vans traditionally produced some interesting motive power pairings in the 1950s and 60s, and the train was a source of interest until newspaper traffic ended in June, 1988. Having just passed South Points, a pair of Manchester Newton Heath Black Fives make a stirring sight as they gather speed past Dringhouses in the 1950s. *(Ernest Sanderson)*

# SHORT MEMORIES

**Summer, 1960:** The 7.50pm Kings Cross-Newcastle Forth express goods accelerated by 45 minutes, named The Tees-Tyne Freighter, retimed to leave London at 8.10pm and runs, stopping only for crew change at Peterborough, to passing York station at an average speed of 43.4mph. Arriving Skelton Yard at 1.5am, it is allowed 55 minutes for examination and detachment of wagons for Selby, Harrogate and Scarborough. There is also a southbound service named The Kings Cross Freighter.

**12.8.60:** J20 0-6-0 64692 of March depot arrives with a goods from Doncaster, returning light engine about an hour later.

**Vintage views at Dringhouses:**
**Above:** An ex-LNER A5 4-6-2T and a BR Standard class 3 2-6-2T make unusual partners as they run light past South Points and head for York in the 1950s.
**Below:** In the late 1940s, LNER D49/2 4-4-0 No.2727 *The Quorn* passes Dringhouses on its way out of York with a stopping train formed of delightfully ancient wooden coaches. The engine has Lentz rotary cam valve gear. *(Both Ernest Sanderson)*

# SHORT MEMORIES

**15.5.61:** Glasgow Polmadie Britannia 70050 *Firth of Clyde* leaves York with the 7.15am to Leeds on this day and again on 18th May.

**8.6.61:** The Royal Train carrying the Queen and the Duke of Edinburgh for the wedding of the Duke and Duchess of Kent at York Minster is worked from Kings Cross to York and back from Malton to London by A4 60028 *Walter K. Wigham*. Special trains for other guests are worked by 60003 *Andrew K. McCosh* and 60015 *Quicksilver*.

**20.6.61:** B16/2 61455 leaves platorm 6 with the 5.16pm express to Hull, a regular turn for its class.

**Above:** One of York's best known B1s, No.61018 *Gnu*, brings a lightweight express, probably the 8.15am from Doncaster, past Dringhouses on 29th October, 1962. Holgate reception sidings are on the right.
**Below:** The rarest of all beasts - a clean WD. Thornaby-based 90072 appears to be ex-works while plodding southwards past Dringhouses with an unfitted express goods on 2nd April, 1962.

Above: The classic lines of the A4s are seen to good effect in this view of No.60019 *Bittern* heading an Up express under 'Dickie Bridge' - a footbridge popular with photographers - and through Holgate platforms on 1st September, 1962.

Right: Viewed from a diesel multiple unit approaching York, B1 No.61031 *Reedbuck* passes Holgate Up excursion platform with a partly fitted express goods on 7th March, 1963.

Below: Holgate reception sidings are still used for staging freight and departmental trains though of course today they are electrified. Back on 7th May, 1962, the sole occupant was a Down van train headed by V2 No.60854.

**Above: Holgate platforms were opened in 1860 and were used primarily for race traffic until about 1939. Although mostly disused for 24 years(the RCTS railtour on page 16 called there), they were still well cared for, complete with attractive gardens on the Up side slopes, until being removed in 1964. They also provided photographers with a good vantage point, as seen by this view of spotless A3 No.60067 *Ladas* at the head of a southbound express on 1st September, 1962.**

HOLGATE BRIDGE - Watering facilities for locomotives are provided for Nos.1 and 2 Down Reception lines and the Down Goods line at Holgate Bridge. The supply pipe is fixed on the footbridge and hoggers placed to serve each of the above lines.

The hoggers are fitted with balance weights to ensure them being clear of the load gauges when not in use. When the hoggers are pulled down into the tenders, they will be held in these positions by catches, and when the watering is completed the catches must be released by pulling the chains provided, thus allowing the hoggers to return clear of the loading gauges. *Eastern Region Northern Area Sectional Appendix, 1968.*

**Right: Regular York J27 0-6-0 No. 65894 (now preserved as NER No.2392) takes water from one of the hoggers fixed to Dickie Bridge. The date is 3rd May, 1962 and 65894 is probably on pilot duty in the Holgate area.**

Above: Yet to receive a name, A1 No.60129 (later *Guy Mannering*) hauls a train of teak-bodied coaches beneath the magnificent NER slotted signals which protected the southern approach to Holgate Junction until replaced by colour lights in 1951, two years after this picture was taken.

Centre: York's prime position on the East Coast main line means that some of the country's most glamorous expresses have called or passed through. This is how the Edinburgh-Kings Cross Flying Scotsman looked in 1964 - Deltic-hauled by No.D9009 *Alycidon* and sporting the famous winged thistle headboard.

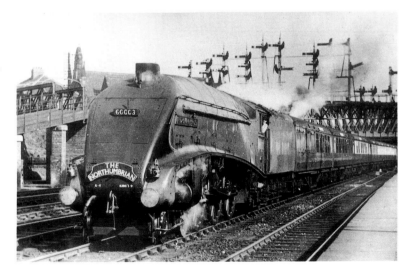

Bottom: A Newcastle-Kings Cross express of the 1950s and 60s was The Northumbrian, seen passing through Holgate with A4 No.60003 *Andrew K. McCosh* in charge. The ramp on the left provided access to the Down excursion platform and was removed in the early 1950s. (*All Ernest Sanderson*)

# SHORT MEMORIES

**8.8.61:** Standard 4MT 2-6-4T 80029, all the way from Ardrossan, is noted on York shed.

**11.9.61:** Train departure sheets posted at York station for the winter timetable up to 17th June, 1962 are experimentally in the 24-hour clock, believed to be, with the exception of boat trains, the first such application on British Railways.

**24.4.62:** Glasgow Polmadie Royal Scot 46121 *Highland Light Infranty, City of Glasgow Regiment* leaves York with the 12.52pm Bristol, having arrived the previous day with the 8.5am from Birmingham.

**17.7.62:** Pioneer A4 60014 *Silver Link* receives attention in the York shed repair shop.

Above: The Cliffe-Uddingston cement train brought Southern Region Birmingham/Sulzer Type 3(Class 33) diesels to York where they handed over to steam or an English Electric Type 4. They usually double-headed, as seen here with Nos.D6573 and D6578 working the southbound train past the trim Holgate gardens on 9th April, 1962.

Below: The iron bridge carrying Holgate Road over the south approaches to York station is such a prominent landmark that it almost marks a gateway between South and North. The first bridge was rebuilt in 1877 to make room for more tracks, while the present one was built in 1911 to accommodate trams on the road above. Coming under the bridge with an express from Scarborough to the London Midland Region on 1st September, 1962 was B16/3 No.61472.

Above: B1 No.61128 approaches York station with the 8.15am from Doncaster on 4th April, 1962 having just passed beneath Holgate bridge. The train has also just negotiated Holgate Junction where the freight avoiding lines through York Yards head off to the right.

Below: Heading south from York station, past the south shed with an empty stock train on 30th March, 1962 was Darlington-based WD 2-8-0 No.90445.

**Summer, 1962:** Thornaby-based English Electric Type 3 diesels now covering a number of Teesside-York freights, some taking over from Sulzer Type 2s and many accompanied by brake tenders to improve braking on unfitted trains.

**Summer, 1962:** Brush Type 2 diesels begin working the 9.38am Saturday Sheffield Midland-York service and 1pm return as English Electric Type 3s take over Hull freights from K3 2-6-0s.

The summer, 1957 timetable saw over 140 weekday passenger trains booked to depart from York in the space of 24 hours.
    They included 18 to Kings Cross, 17 to Leeds, 15 to Scarborough, 12 to Newcastle, 8 to Newcastle via the Durham coast, 8 to Hull via Market Weighton, 7 to Harrogate, 5 to Edinburgh, 4 each to Glasgow Queen Street, Bristol, Sheffield Midland and Doncaster, 3 each to Colchester and Normanton, 2 each to Manchester Victoria, Tyne Commission Quay, Liverpool Exchange, Bradford Forster Square, Swindon, Birmingham New St., Darlington, and Whitby, and one each to Bournemouth West, Lowestoft, Cardiff, Hull via Selby, Stockton-on-Tees, West Hartlepool, Filey via Market Weighton, Sunderland via Newcastle, Selby, Saltburn, Aberdeen and Fort William.

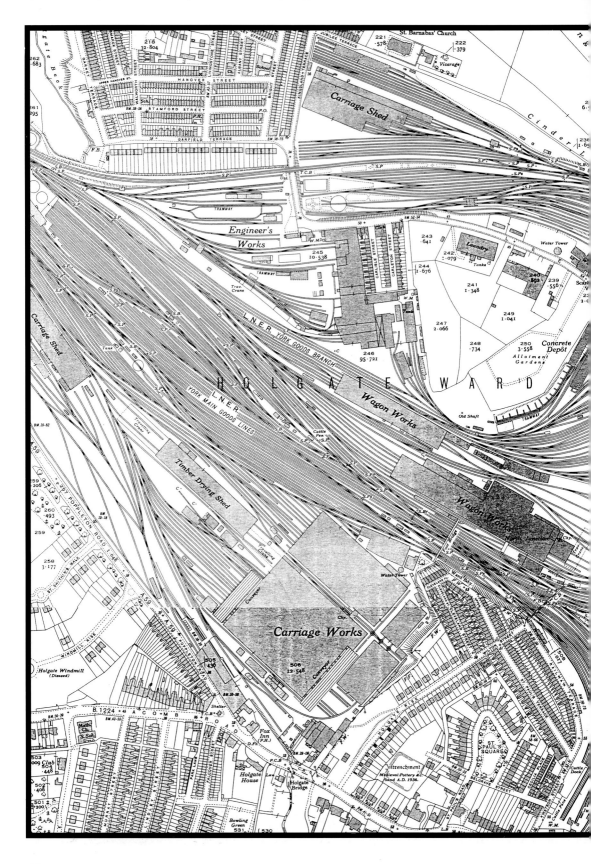

30

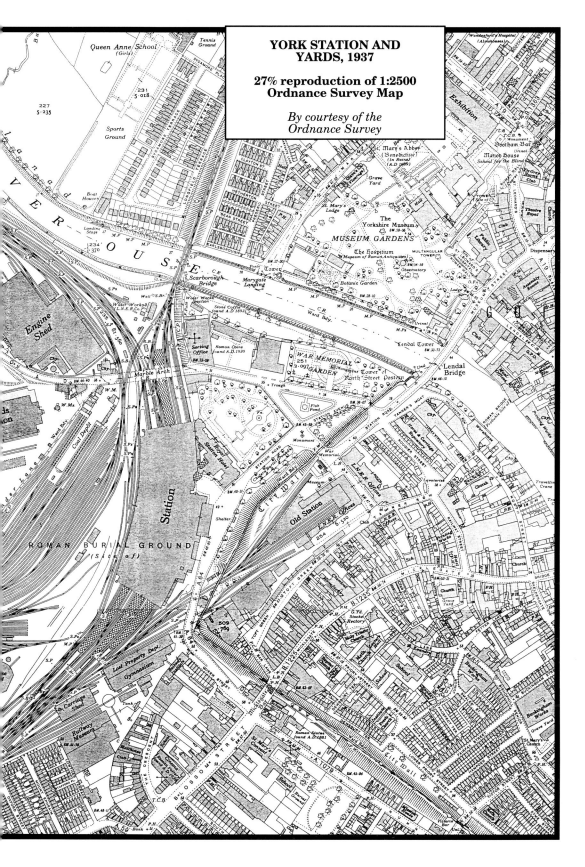

YORK STATION AND
YARDS, 1937

27% reproduction of 1:2500
Ordnance Survey Map

*By courtesy of the
Ordnance Survey*

Top: The Capitals Limited ran non-stop between Kings Cross and Edinburgh from 1949 but was speeded up and renamed The Elizabethan in 1953 to celebrate the coronation of Queen Elizabeth 11. A4 No.60011 *Empire of India* eases the southbound Capitals past Loco Yard signal box, the world's biggest manual box with 295 levers until its abolition in 1951. Behind the signal gantry is a footbridge leading to the signal box and loco depot.

Centre: A1 No.60153 *Flamboyant* was a York engine for its entire 14-year life. Pictured new and still un-named, No.60153 also had the unfortunate distinction of being the first of the class to be withdrawn. *(Both Ernest Sanderson)*

Bottom: With the old Queen Street erecting shops on the right, Royal Scot No.46141 *The North Staffordshire Regiment* gets the 12.43 Newcastle-Bristol on its way on 9th May, 1962.

Top: A rare 1949 view taken from Loco Yard signal box of the unique D49/4 4-4-0 No.62768 *The Morpeth*. The Starbeck-based loco was rebuilt in 1942 with two inside cylinders of the same pattern as those on the ex-Great Central D11 4-4-0s. From the right are Queen Street shed, the old No.1 erecting shop, and tracks leading through the city wall to the 1841 station. (*Ernest Sanderson*)

Centre: One of the Queen Street machine shops in use as a Road Motor Engineer's garage on 31st January, 1961, with the Dormobile vans of the day present alongside a railway horse box. By 1994 the building was a covered car park.

Bottom: In 1926, a neighbouring shop became a museum which lasted until the end of 1973 when it closed in preparation for the new National Railway Museum. LNWR 2-2-2 *Columbine* and GNR 4-4-2 No.251, seen on 7th February, 1962, were among locos displayed at Queen Street. The building was demolished in 1979. (*both by courtesy of British Rail*)

York shed had a notable fleet of A2 Pacifics until they were either withdrawn or transferred to Scotland at the end of 1962. The differences between Peppercorn-designed A2 No.60526 *Sugar Palm* (above) and Thompson A2/3 No.60512 *Steady Aim* (below) are readily visible as they wait on stand-by for diesel failures at Queen Street shed on 9th April, 1962 and 18th April, 1961 respectively.

Top: York South sheds were closed and only the straight shed remained in use on 2nd May, 1963, for storing engines which included A1 No.60146 *Peregrine* and WD 2-8-0 No.90424.

Centre: Gas, made from oil at the railway's own gas works in Leeman Road, was delivered to stations and yards for such purposes as lighting in special cylinder wagons, many of which were stored disused at the south shed on 30th March, 1962. The larger roundhouse is on the left and a DMU with collision damage is in the centre road.

Bottom: Among the original B16s stored at the straight shed in February, 1961 were ex-LMS 3F 0-6-0T No.47556 and J72 0-6-0T No.69016. The antique-looking J72 was in fact only 10 years old, being one of a batch built at Darlington by BR to the NER's 1898 design.

Top: This delightful scene was captured on 8th September, 1962 but the diesels were taking over and A4 No.60025 *Falcon*, at platform 9 with an Up express, would soon be withdrawn. Brush Type 2 No.D5835 was piloting B1 No.61003 *Gazelle* on the 12.28 to Doncaster.

Right: Sharing express passenger duty, a pair of BR/Sulzer Type 2 (class 24) diesels, No.D5015 leading, prepare to leave platform 14 with a train for the Western Region. *(Ernest Sanderson)*

Below: Coming in from the south, Doncaster-based A1 No.60157 *Great Eastern* approaches platform 14 with the 9am from Kings Cross on 2nd May, 1963.

Top: The short-lived Raven Pacifics(LNER Class A2) were named after cities served by the NER and this was No.2402 *City of York* at platform 8 South in pre-war LNER days. These five locos, actually introduced in 1924, were all withdrawn by 1936. *(Cecil Ord)*

Centre: In October, 1964, the preserved LNER Gresley K4 2-6-0 No.3442 *The Great Marquess* shared a railtour to the North East with preserved A3 *Flying Scotsman*. It has just arrived at platform 15 with the return train and is about to hand it back to the Pacific. *(Stephen Chapman)*

Below: Moments after the top picture was taken, ex-NER Raven 4-4-4T No.1326 drew up alongside *City of York*. Like all NER passenger engines, the 4-4-4Ts were fitted with Westinghouse air pumps for working air-braked stock and were rebuilt from 1931 onwards as Class A8 4-6-2Ts *(Cecil Ord)*

# SHORT MEMORIES

**1.9.62:** J94 0-6-0ST 68078 of Langwith Junction is on shed.

**October, 1962:** British Railways announces plans for reshaping its main workshops. York carriage works to continue building and repairing coaching stock and 2,180 workforce increased by 600. Wagon works to close but container repairs to continue at the carriage works.

Top: The centre road between platforms 14 and 15 was known as the Engine Line but on 25th April, 1963, K1 2-6-0 No.62063 was working through with a train of pallet vans loaded with sweets from Rowntree's factory.

Centre: In 1960, J72 0-6-0Ts used as station pilots at York and Newcastle were repainted in NER green. York's 68736 takes a breather at platform 11 on 7th May, 1961. Within a few months it had been replaced by 204hp 0-6-0 diesel shunters and sent to join its classmate at Newcastle where it worked on until 1963.

Bottom: Having backed onto its Manchester train in platform 10 on the same day, was Agecroft Black Five No.44781, a regular visitor to York at the time.

Above: Another one of York's regular J72 pilots was No.68677, seen on the Engine Line between platforms 14 and 15 on 7th February, 1961. The extra canopied platform in the background was the fruit dock. All York's J72s were either withdrawn or transferred away by the end of 1961.

Below: Another regular visitor to York from across the Pennines was Liverpool Bank Hall's un-named Patriot 4-6-0 No.45517, which often worked the Liverpool Exchange-Newcastle express as far as York, a duty it shared with Jubilees 45698 *Mars* and 45717 *Dauntless*. *(Ernest Sanderson)*

Left: The Royal Scots were among prime ex-LMS power which came to York until the mid-1960s. No.46141 *The North Staffordshire Regiment* ambles between platform 16 and the fruit dock while making its way from the North shed to take over the 12.43 Newcastle-Bristol on 9th May, 1962. Deltic No.D9002 lurks in the background.

Centre: Platforms 15 and 16 had still to be built when Midland 4-4-0 No.359 was caught leaving platform 11. The engine shed on the left was demolished in the 1930s to make way for the new platforms. *(Cecil Ord)*

Below: One of York's most prolific cross-country expresses was the 10.8am to Bournemouth which often included Southern Region green coaches. It ran via the Great Central main line to Banbury, Oxford and Reading, and is seen on 14th January, 1963 awaiting departure behind V2 No.60828. Loco-hauled InterCity trains to and from the south coast could still be seen at York in 1994.

Above: Another view of the Bournemouth train, booked to leave York at 10.18 when photographed on 29th May, 1961 in charge of B16/3 No.61468 which would work as far as Sheffield Victoria.

Right: The Scarborough Flyer was another prolific express, running during the summer between Kings Cross and Scarborough. B16/3 No.61444 has just arrived at platform 8 South with the London-bound train on 8th September, 1962, and is about to hand over to V2 No.60803. English Electric Type 4 No.D276 is hauling one of the SR green horse boxes popularised by the Hornby Dublo model.

Owing to the length and curvature of York station, the ends of its platforms were equipped with electric bells to expedite the starting of trains and the following Appendix instruction applied: Guards-in-charge of trains must use these bells to indicate to the front guard that the train is ready to start, and the latter, on hearing the bell, may signal the train away in the usual manner.

Where there is only one guard with a train, drivers may accept the ringing of a bell as a signal to start. instead of a green flag or light referred to in Rule 141.

Above: This was the kind of atmosphere which could be savoured from the comfort of the platform 14 buffet on chilly days. On 28th March, 1961, Britannia Pacific No.70036 *Boadicea* has just arrived at platform 14 with an express from the eastern counties while Jubilee No.45717 *Dauntless* is on the express from Liverpool Exchange. Platform 14 was added in 1900 and platforms 15/16 in 1937/8.

Below: Preserved A3 No.4472 *Flying Scotsman* is today a familiar sight hauling special trains on the main line. It had just begun its life in preservation when arriving at platform 15 with a railtour for the north in April, 1964. *(Stephen Chapman collection)*

## SHORT MEMORIES

**17.11.62:** Edinburgh Haymarket A2 60536 *Trimbush* is a rare visitor to York.

**24.2.63:** Hull Dairycoates 350hp diesel shunter 12122 is noted on shed, probably on its way to or from Darlington Works.

**4th April, 1963:** Deltic D9002 is named *King's Own Yorkshire Light Infantry* in a ceremony at York station.

**Summer, 1963:** Eight 9F 2-10-0s are transferred to York from the Southern and Western Regions. They are 92005/6/205/6/11/21/31/9.

**20.7.63:** Notable visitors include Consett K1 2-6-0 62022 and Motherwell-based Fairburn 2-6-4T 42122.

Top: Branches Yard, on the west side of York station, is now just a fading memory, the site being occupied by a major servicing centre for signalling equipment, the new signal box opened in 1989, and car parks. It was still handling traffic for local depots along the various branches out of York on 2nd August, 1962 when BR Class 3 2-6-0 No.77013 was setting off for its Scarborough home with a return pick-up goods.

Centre: Shunting a corner of the yard known as South View on 15th May, 1962 was J27 No.65890.

Below: Breathtaking light effects and dramatic sunsets were a regular feature of the western sky over Branches Yard and South sheds(left of picture). J27 No.65874 is bathed in afternoon sunlight while starting empty pallet vans on their way to Rowntree's factory. The raised wagons in the right background are on Leeman Road coal drops.

When the new signalling was commissioned in 1951, the biggest and most advanced route relay interlocking system in the world, controlling over 33 miles of track, replaced seven manual signal boxes. From then until the present solid state system controlling over 200 miles of track was inaugurated on 11th May, 1989, it was controlled from a huge power box situated above platform 14.

Top: The box looms large above V2 No.60905 as it starts a Bristol-Newcastle express from platform 14 on 7th March, 1963.

Centre: This interior view of the 50ft panel on 25th May, 1962 illustrates the extent of the York station layout at the time.

Bottom: The complex track layout featured some specialist pointwork and this single slip at Leeman Road Junction includes a switch diamond with the switch set for the road to the North shed. On 25th April, 1963, Ivatt Class 4 2-6-0 No.43014 was about to pass by on its way into Branches Yard with a through freight from Scarborough or Hull.

Top: Because of its historic and architectural status, the basic structure of York station has changed little since this picture was taken of the main entrance on 14th April, 1961. However, plenty around it has, not least the Leeds and Harrogate fares of 4s 6d(22.5p) and 4s 3d (21.25p) respectively, advertised on the portico. Most striking, though, is the lack of road traffic. The Royal Station Hotel, sold into private ownership in 1983, is on the right.

Centre: Looking from the portico into the outer concourse on 5th February, 1962. *(Both by courtesy of British Rail)*

Bottom: Looking south across the rooftops of the 1841 station from the 1906 NER headquarters on 18th May, 1962. Beyond the city wall in the centre are the Queen Street erecting shops and, right, the roof of the present station. Just inside the walls are, centre, the Sack Warehouse and the old station itself.

The roof in the centre foreground is that of the Georgian station building while on the right is the hotel built in 1853. The wooden huts on the left, which latterly housed the signal and telegraph department, were put up by the NER in the 1890s to alleviate the shortage of office accommodation which led to the main HQ being built. In 1994, all the buildings were still used as railway offices except the huts which were demolished in the 1980s.

Above: Towards the left of Queen Street sidings, seen here on 18th May, 1962, was York's first, temporary station used by the YNMR between 1839 and 1841, while the GNE main line to Darlington would have passed almost at right angles to the platforms. Royal Mail Travelling Post Office vans occupy the track leading beneath Queen Street itself as B1 No.61124 arrives at platform 1 with the 8.15am from Doncaster. The 204hp diesel pilot is BR/Gardener(Class 03) No.D2062.

Below: On the opposite side of Queen Street and the city wall to the above picture, was this view of the Sack Warehouse. It was demolished in 1967 to make way for the Hudson House office block. *(Ernest Sanderson)*

# SHORT MEMORIES

**20.7.63:** Locos stored at the South shed include: Stanier Class 3 2-6-2T 40117; Ivatt Class 2 2-6-2Ts 41251/65; Ivatt Class 4 2-6-0 43014; Ivatt Class 2 2-6-0 46473; A1s 60124 *Kenilworth*, 60138 *Boswell*, 60140 *Balmoral*, 60146 *Peregrine*, 60150 *Willbrook*, 60154 *Bon Accord*; V2s 60810/37/77/60911/63; B16s 61434/63; K1 62063; J27s 65844/88; Standard Class 2 2-6-0 78010; Standard Class 3 2-6-2Ts 82026-8; WD 2-8-0s 90424/518/71.

**30.9.63:** Deltic D9005 named *The Prince of Wales's Own Regiment of Yorkshire* in a ceremony at York station.

# LOCOMOTIVES OBSERVED AT YORK

## 9.30am-5.15pm 23rd June, 1962

Ivatt 4MT 2-6-0: 43014/56/128; Fairburn 4MT 2-6-4T 42682; Crab 2-6-0: 42705/95; 4F 0-6-0: 44221; 5MT 4-6-0: 44664/717/805/74/5321/435/85; Jubilee 4-6-0: 45565 *Victoria*/45652 *Hawke*/45661 *Vernon*; 8F 2-8-0: 48060/337/59/71/2; A4 4-6-2: 60007 *Sir Nigel Gresley*/60011 *Empire of India*/60019 *Bittern*/60029 *Woodcock*/60030 *Golden Fleece*; A3 4-6-2: 60051 *Blink Bonny*/60058 *Blair Atholl*/60061 *Pretty Polly*/60083 *Sir Hugo*/60088 *Book Law*/60105 *Victor Wild*/60112 *St. Simon*; A1/1 4-6-2: 60113 *Great Northern*; A1 4-6-2: 60126 *Sir Vincent Raven*/60129 *Guy Mannering*/60138 *Boswell*/60155 *Borderer*; A2/3 4-6-2: 60524 *Herringbone*; V2 2-6-2: 60803/60809 *The Snapper, The East Yorkshire Regiment. The Duke of York's Own*/28/35/60847 *St. Peter's School, York* AD627/56/87/910/36/7/9/48/63/8/82; B1 4-6-0: 61002 *Impala*/61013 *Topi*/61020 *Gemsbok*/61034 *Chiru*/61037 *Jairou*/61039 *Steinbok*/53/62/110/64/205/29/61244 *Strang Steel*/61245 *Murray of Elibank*/54/62/73/305/19/61379 *Mayflower*/88; B16/2 4-6-0: 61437/57/75; B16/3 4-6-0: 61417/34/9/48/72; K3 2-6-0: 61840/67/93/1908/22/85; K1 2-6-0: 62007/9/41/8/9/56/63/5; O1 2-8-0: 63619/30; O4 2-8-0: 63920; O2 2-8-0: 63932/49; J39 0-6-0: 64806/64/7; J27 0-6-0: 65883/5/94; J72 0-6-0T: 69009; 5MT 4-6-0: 73166; 3MT 2-6-0: 77012; 4MT 2-6-4T: 80118; 3MT 2-6-2T: 82026/8/9; WD 2-8-0: 90018/29/31/202/352/80/421/4/94/512/78/663/4/730; 9F 2-10-0: 92135/81; Sulzer Type 4: D14/24/8/32/41/2/68/78/108/12/29/44; English Electric Type 4: D209/37/8/41/5/54/76/80/1/2/3/93/313/9/ 50/1/6/60/8/88/90; BR/Gardener 204hp 0-6-0: D2063/75/112/3/50/1/9; Drewry 204hp 0-6-0: D2269; 350hp 0-6-0: D3071/313/20; Brush Type 2: D5638/55/7/83/803/6; Sulzer Type 3: D6518/35/85; English Electric Type 3: D6731/3/4/7; English Electric Deltic: D9000 *Royal Scots Grey*/D9002 *The King's Own Yorkshire Light Infantry*/6/8/D9009 *Alycidon*/10/4/D9020 *Nimbus*;

**Below: Seen from Queen Street sidings on 6th May, 1962, A3 4-6-2 No.60062 *Minoru* waits to take a parcels train out of platform 1.**

# SHORT MEMORIES

The 12.52pm to Bristol was an interesting cross-country departure which produced engines from as far away as Bristol Barrow Road.

Barrow Road Jubilee No.45682 *Trafalgar*(above) was in charge on 10th May, 1962, while on 2nd April(below) Saltley Black Five No.44920 was being stoked up at platform 3 for the long run ahead.

**1.10.63:** Royal Scots 46118 *Royal Welch Fusilier* (12B) and 46162 *Queen's Westminster Rifleman* (12A) arrive with football specials from Carlisle.

**3.7.64:** Clayton Type 1 diesel D8588, believed to be the first of this new class to visit York, arrives on a Tees Yard-Dringhouses freight.

**17.7.65:** A1s 60129 *Guy Mannering* and 60151 *Midlothian* join the York fleet. V2 60847 *St Peter's School, York* is withdrawn and one of its nameplates presented to the school the following week.

Above: Platform 1 was converted to a dock for loading cars onto car sleeper trains, replacing the facility at the old station when it was abandoned in 1966. Here, V2 2-6-2 No.60853 has just arrived at platform 1 with the 8.15am from Doncaster on 23rd May, 1962.
Left: BR Standard Class 5 4-6-0 No.73015 of Bristol Barrow Road shed waits to leave platform 3 with the 12.52 to Bristol on 16th March, 1961.

Mr. Eric Warcup became a ticket collector at York station in 1959 and recalls the type of work he did in the early 1960s:

"I attended evening classes and after passing rules and regs in ticket examination, I got a trainside ticket collector's post working three shifts.

"My duties consisted of relieving the regular barrier men for meal breaks and working several hours on afternoons on the outward barrier or checking trains in the station.

"On nights we had to check all trains passing through the station to see that people were in the correct class of travel and had valid tickets.

"Most trains stood 10 minutes or more for platform duties and we started in the first class to examine tickets. Anyone with a second class ticket was excessed.

"It was very hectic on Bank Holidays and race days as we had special and relief trains arriving every few minutes and some of the rece-goers would try every trick in the book to avoid paying the correct fare.

"At least two or three times a week when checking night trains we got a passenger without a ticket, no money and no fixed abode so we'd take him off the train and hand him over to the British Transport Police. They would take a statement off you and you would have to go to court the next morning to give evidence, unless the passenger pleaded guilty in which case you could go home to bed, which wasn't often."

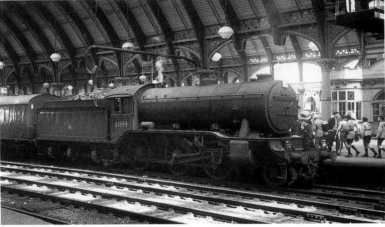

Top: York's Standard Class 3 2-6-0 No.77012 was regularly deployed on officers' and engineers' inspection duties. On 10th May, 1962, 77012 was receiving attention from its driver at the south end of platform 9 while coupled to a pair of officers' saloons, the second being 6-wheeler No.E900269E.

Centre: K3 2-6-0 No.61899 calls at platform 8 North on 23rd August, 1962 with special train 1Z04. Behind the party of scouts is the old tea room. A staff canteen until the late 1960s, it then became a BR railway relics shop and in 1994 housed the Railriders' World model railway.

Bottom: Looking north from the station footbridge as Standard Class 5 No.73160 passes through on the Up Main with non-stop excursion 1Z02 from Scarborough on 29th July, 1962.

Above: With the Harrogate and Darlington bays, platforms 12 and 13, on the left, now-preserved Jubilee No.45690 *Leander*, then of Bristol Barrow Road, rolls an excursion through the station on 20th April, 1961 while a Metro-Cammell DMU waits at platform 8 North.

Below: The crust of grime covering A3 No.60103 *Flying Scotsman* hardly becomes the world's most famous locomotive as it stands at platform 9 with a northbound express on 8th August, 1962. It could hardly have impressed the youngsters taking part in a railway induction course.

Summer Saturdays saw a procession of extra trains passing through York on their way to Scarborough, Bridlington or the Butlin's camp at Filey.

Top: Royal Scot No.46115 *Scots Guardsman* - another ex-LMS 4-6-0 which has survived into preservation - takes the Scarborough line with train 1Z38 on 2nd June, 1963.

Bottom: The stock of a charter train to the British Oil and Cake Mills at Selby is on its way to Clifton carriage sidings for servicing behind Jubilee No.45681 *Aboukir* on 30th March, 1963.

Centre: Up to the end of the 1950s, York had a large allocation of Worsdell J71 0-6-0Ts to complement its ten J72s on pilot duties. In this 1930s view, LNER J71 No.1167 was No.3 pilot.

*(Cecil Ord)*

# SHORT MEMORIES

**27.11.65:** B1 61306 hauls the 08.14 and 17.40 to Hull via Market Weighton and the 12.08 parcels and 19.35 passenger from Hull on the last day of services. The last train of all, the 21.45 to Hull, is a 6-car DMU with a Cravens 2-car unit leading and carrying a farewell headboard.

**31.12.65:** A1 60145 *Saint Mungo* works the last booked steam express passenger train on the East Coast main line north of York, the 18.30 relief to Newcastle. It returns later with the empty stock.

Above: The Snapper - as Darlington-based V2 No.60809 *The Snapper*. The East Yorkshire Regiment, The Duke of York's Own was better known, was an appropriate and regular visitor, mingling with York's own large allocation of the class. Here, it is seen competently tackling the tricky start from platform 9 with a northbound express on 29th July, 1962.

Left: The English Electric prototype Class 50 diesel No.DP2 had a regular turn through York in the 1960s, as seen on 20th May, 1967. Two months later, DP2 was written off at Thirsk when it crashed at 80mph into the Cliffe-Uddingston cement train which had become derailed on the adjacent slow line. Seven people were killed while DP2 languished, sheeted over, in York shed yard before being towed back to its makers at Vulcan Foundry for dismantling. *(Brian Myland)*

Mr. Sydney Martin, who worked at York station but was transferred elsewhere at the time of the bombing on 29th April, 1942, recalls how colleague Bill Jameson, faced his terrifying night's duty:

"The Night Aberdonian with a Pacific on had just stopped in platform 9 when thump, thump, thump, the bombs fell and the south end of the station was devastated.

"Bill helped passengers as much as possible. He then told Loco Yard box to put the pilot engine on the rear of the long train. The signalman set the points and when the engine arrived Bill coupled it to the train.

"He got the driver to gently pull the coaches back to Holgate Bridge, having uncoupled those which were on fire. Bill and his mate then took some more coaches from platforms 14 and 15 to a safe place, and then tried to assist without losing any more time.

"Staff were given awards but Bill did not get one because when an official came the next morning to ask who did what, he had gone off duty and was forgotten.

"During the war, York station had shunters at each corner - a head shunter, an assistant and pilot loco for drawing out trains and transferring vehicles.

"At the peak of war traffic it also had a station master who always wore a silk hat and frock coat, three assistants, 16 inspectors, 30 foremen, a locomotive inspector, 75 passenger guards, platform porters and porters for dealing with parcels, postal and fish traffic, carriage and wagon staff, lampmen, police, a Services Transport Officer, and a team of ticket collectors under a foreman collector - quite different from the present few staff.

"There were many trains, freight and passenger, yet they got through - some of the expresses with 18 coaches on. Coal was switched to rail from sea so there were many extra coal trains. They were re-manned on the riverside line at Clifton in the Up direction, and on platform 14 in the Down direction.

"In those days there was also a compressed air tube system between the station Outer Office and the Headquarters Telegraph Office which was very busy with messages passing in both directions. The Telegraph Office was then mainly on the old ticker instrument which showed incoming messages with a fast moving needle - the letter `A' was one left, one right, S.O.S. was three left, three right, three left, just like Morse code."

Top: York station has been the set for railway scenes in a number of films. This was the Tea Room Square entrance, which led directly to the buffer stop ends of bay platforms 4-7, on 19th June, 1980 when it was disguised as London Victoria for the making of Chariots of Fire. *(Stephen Chapman)*

Centre: Early 1963 saw possibly the second harshest winter in living memory so far. Heavy snow followed by severe frosts, night after night, put many diesels out of action and some services, including the 8.14am to Hull reverted to steam. Surrounded by steam and snow at platform 6 on 2nd February while on this working was York B1 No.61062. A Cravens DMU is snowbound in platform 5.

Bottom: The 8.14am to Hull again, on 19th February with Hull Dairycoates B1 No.61080 in charge. Composed mostly of vans with only a couple of passenger coaches, this train was allowed generous station stops for offloading mail and parcels, being timed to take 87 minutes for the 42-mile journey.

# SHORT MEMORIES

**19.3.66:** 60145 *Saint Mungo*, the last A1, works a freight from York to Healey Mills.

**April, 1966:** *Saint Mungo*, now withdrawn, temporarily restored to traffic as Standard 2-6-0 77012 returns to York following a spell at Bradford. Also returning is Ivatt 2-6-0 43055 as 43014 and 43126 are withdrawn.

Right: The Smarty Express - as the trip from Rowntrees was known - snakes across Waterworks Crossing and into Branches Yard behind J27 0-6-0 No.65894 at lunchtime on 22nd January, 1962. Centre: Seen during the course of renewal on 16th October, 1961, Water-works Crossing took its name from the pumphouse in the background which drew the railway's water supply from the river below. (By courtesy of British Rail) Below: On 1st May, 1962 Class A2/3 No.60500 *Edward Thompson* (named after its designer) brings a short parcels train over the crossing. The crossing was removed in the mid-1970s, enabling platform 14 to be extended.

Top: Ivatt 2-6-0 No.43055 comes off Scarborough bridge over the River Ouse and heads for Branches Yard with the returning Market Weighton pick-up on 11th May, 1961.

Bottom: A1 No.60139 *Sea Eagle* makes a vigorous start from York station on a cold 26th February, 1963 and rounds the curve to Clifton with a Newcastle-bound express.

Centre: Coming the other way with an Up 1950s express is A3 No.60075 *St. Frusquin*, still to be rebuilt with a double chimney. *(Stephen Chapman collection)*

York North motive power depot, known to many railwaymen as Clifton shed, was established in 1877 when it consisted of three roundhouses under a single roof. An extra roundhouse was added in 1915 but the shed was badly damaged by the air raid of 29th April, 1942. In 1957/8 two roundhouses were replaced by a straight repair shop with such up to date heavy repair facilities as overhead cranes, illuminated inspection pits and a wheel drop pit. The remaining two roundhouses were reroofed and updated.
From nationalisation, York engines bore the famous 50A shedcode until summer, 1967 when the shed became part of the Leeds Division and adopted the far less prestigous 55B. The engines stood alongside the shed on 8th June, 1963 were just a fraction of those ranged along the depot's vast yard. Along with WD 2-8-0s were B1 No.61229 and J27 No.65894.

# LOCOMOTIVES ALLOCATED TO YORK

## Summer, 1950

A1 4-6-2: 60121 *Silurian*/60138 *Boswell*/60140 *Balmoral*/60146 *Peregrine* / 60153 *Flamboyant;* A2/2 4-6-2: 60501 *Cock o' the North* / 60502 *Earl Marischal* / 60503 *Lord President*; A2/3 60522 *Straight Deal*/60524 *Herringbone*; A2 4-6-2: 60526 *Sugar Palm*; V2 2-6-2: 60837/9/43/47 *St. Peter's School, York* AD627/56/64/ 901/4/7/18/25/9/33/4/41/6/54/60/1/2/3/8/74/5/6/7/8/9/81/2; B1 4-6-0: 61015 *Duiker*/61016 *Inyala*/61020 *Gemsbok* /61038 *Blacktail*/71/84/115/1239/88/1337; B16/1 4-6-0: 61416/9/22/3/4/6/30/6/41/3/50/1/2/6/9/60/2/5/6/73/4/7; B16/2 4-6-0: 61421/35/7/8/55/7/75; B16/3 4-6-0: 61417/8/20/34/9/44/8/9/53/4/61/3/4/7/8/ 72/6; D20 4-4-0: 62369; D49 4-4-0: 62726 *The Meynell* /62727 *The Quorn* /62736 *The Bramham Moor* /62740 *The Bedale*/62742 *The Braes of Derwent* /62744 *The Holderness*/62745 *The Hurworth* /62759 *The Craven* /62760 *The Cotswold* / 62761 *The Derwent;* Q5 0-8-0: 63270; J21 0-6-0: 65043/75; J24 0-6-0: 65619; J25 0-6-0: 65656/79/5700/8/23; J27 0-6-0: 65845/9/61/83/5/8/90/4; J94 0-6-0ST: 68017/31/2/ 40/4/6/61; Y8 0-4-0T: 68091; Y1 4wVBT: 68152; J71 0-6-0T: 68230/8/ 40/6/50/3/75/ 80/2/6/92/3/4/7/310/3; J77 0-6-0T: 68436; J72 0-6-0T: 68695/9/715/22/6/35/9/41/5 /69020; WD 2-8-0: 90056/69/99/100/200/35/424/32/511/ 8/609/70. Total: 173.

Above: The early 1960s saw plenty of Britannia Pacifics visiting York with freight and passenger trains from such places as March and Immingham. On 14th January, 1963 Nos.70036 *Boadicea* and 70034 *Thomas Hardy* were to be found parked alongside the shed.

Below: Alongside the shed on 14th January, 1963 was Fowler 2-6-4T No.42327, a visitor from Wigan Springs Branch, with Toton-based 9F 2-10-0 No.92059 behind. An English Electric Type 4 diesel stands in the entrance to the repair shop.

**October, 1964:** British Railways announces a £200,000 modernisation programme for York carriage works which will be responsible for building all new coaching stock as well as repairs. Under construction at this time are 216 London-Brighton express electric multiple unit vehicles.

**October, 1964:** British Railways publishes new proposals for closure of the York-Harrogate line.

**11.10.64:** Southern Region Merchant Navy Pacific 35007 *Aberdeen Commonwealth* reaches York with a railtour from the West Midlands.

The breakdown crane allocated to York in the 1960s was a relatively small one for a depot of its size and importance. Steam crane No.331158 had a 35-ton lifting capacity and covered an area from Ferrybridge in the south, to Northallerton in the north. It could also be requested by Control to work as far south as Doncaster and Sheffield Victoria.

# LOCOMOTIVES ALLOCATED TO YORK

## Autumn, 1961

Fairburn 4MT 2-6-4T: 42085; Stanier 4MT 2-6-4T: 42553; Ivatt 4MT 2-6-0: 43014/55/6/71/96; Ivatt 2MT 2-6-0: 46480/1; Midland 3F 0-6-0T: 47239; LMS 0-6-0T: 47421/48/556; A1 4-6-2: 60121 *Silurian*/60138 *Boswell*/60140 *Balmoral*/60141 *Abbotsford*/60146 *Peregrine*/60150 *Willbrook*/60153 *Flamboyant*/60154 *Bon Accord*; A2/2 4-6-2: 60502 *Earl Marischal*; A2/3 4-6-2: 60512 *Steady Aim*/60515 *Sun Stream*/60516 *Hycilla*/60518 *Tehran*/60522 *Straight Deal*/60524 *Herringbone*; A2 4-6-2: 60526 *Sugar Palm*; V2 2-6-2: 60810/28/31/7/9/42/60847 *St. Peter's School, York* AD627/55/6/64/76/7/8/9/87/95/ 907/18/25/35/9/41/54/61/3/8/74/5/7/81/2; B1 4-6-0: 61002 *Impala*/61018 *Gnu*/61020 *Gemsbok*/61021 *Reitbok*/61031 *Reedbuck*/61039 *Steinbok*/49/53/62/8/9/71/84/6/1198/1229/ 61240 *Harry Hinchcliffe*/73/6/88/ 91/1319/37/88; B16/1 4-6-0: 61419/22/3/5/31/6/43/50/1/ 2/9/60/6/73; B16/2 4-6-0: 61421/35/7/8/55/7/75; B16/3 4-6-0:61417/8/20/34/9/44/8/9/53/ 4/61/3/4/7/8/72/6; K1 2-6-0: 62005/9/46/7/9/56/7/61/3/5; J27 0-6-0: 65874/83/5/7/90/4; J94 0-6-0ST: 68046/61; J72 0-6-0T: 68677/86/7/736/9003/8/16; 3MT 2-6-0: 77012; WD 2-8-0: 90026/45/424/67/518/663; English Electric Type 4(Class 40): D252/3/4/8/9/75/ 6/81/2/3/4/5; BR/Gardener 204hp 0-6-0: D2046/62/3/5/6/75/103/10/1/2/3/51/8/9/60/1; Drewry 204hp 0-6-0: D2245/68/9/70; 350hp 0-6-0: D3070/1/3235/7/8/9/40/ 3313/4/5/8/9/20/3872/4/3940/6; Departmental 4w diesel: 84. Total: 203(154 Steam, 49 diesel)

## November, 1966

V2 2-6-2: 60831; B1 4-6-0: 61012 *Puku*/61017 *Bushbuck*/61019 *Nilghal*/61021 *Reitbok*/61035 *Pronghorn*/1199/216/61238 *Leslie Runciman*/1303/19/37; K1 2-6-0: 62012/28/42/6/65; 3MT 2-6-0: 77002/12; 9F 2-10-0: 92231/9; English Electric Type 4: D241/3/4/9/52/3/70/1/6/ 8/80/1/3/4/5/6/345/6/8/56/86/ 94/5/6/7; Brush Type 4: D1100/1/2/3/4/1989/90/1/2/3/4/5/6/7/8/9; BR/Gardener 204hp 0-6-0(Class 03): D2046/51/2/3/4/62/3/6/75/81/111/2/3/51/8/9/ 60; Drewry 204hp 0-6-0(Class 04): D2231/45/68/9/70; 350hp 0-6-0: D3076/237/ 8/9/40/314/ 5/9/20/872/4/ 946; Sulzer Type 2(Class 24): D5096/8/ 9/5100/76/7/8; English Electric Type 3: D6784/5/6/ 7/8/9/90/1/2/3/4/5/ 834/5/6; Engineer's Dept 4w diesel: 84. Total: 119 (21 steam, 98 diesel)

The steam age had only nine months left to run so far as York was concerned but the roundhouse was still well stocked with a good variety of engines on 13th September, 1966. Present were B1 4-6-0 No.61319, K1 2-6-0 No.62028, V2 2-6-2 No.60805, 9F 2-10-0s Nos.92205 and 92239, and J27 0-6-0 No.65823.

Above: York's best known J27, No.65894, was still active inside the shed on 13th September, 1966. After steam finished, the roundhouse was used mainly for stabling departmental vehicles and a number of privately preserved steam locos as well as the odd diesel. It closed altogether in 1973 for conversion to the National Railway Museum's main exhibition hall.

Centre: Also in the shed on the same day were B1 No.61319, V2 No.60831 (soon to be York's last) and Ivatt Class 4 No.43123, all without work.

Bottom: York roundhouse in the 1930s before it was destroyed by Hitler's bombs. Hull and Barnsley Railway Stirling Class N13 0-6-2T No.8485 is present alongside a D20 4-4-0, probably No.1026. (Ernest Sanderson)

Right: The North Eastern Region Chief Civil Engineer's depart-ment had its own shunter for working the Leeman Road permanent way yard. Ruston and Hornsby 4-wheel diesel No.84, seen in the roundhouse on 6th July, 1969, succeeded Class Y1 Sentinel vertical boilered steam loco No.68152 in the 1950s. *(Brian Myland)*

# SHORT MEMORIES

**Spring, 1966:** Brush Type 4(Class 47) diesels now being allocated to York in increasing numbers and include brand new D1990-9.

**2.5.66:** Leeman Road coal depot closes.

**July, 1966:** Ex-WR Type 3s D6819/20/2/3/4/ 5/6/7/ 8/9/30 are among diesels transferred to York with many more of the class following over subsequent months. *Saint Mungo* is withdrawn for the last time.

**Summer, 1966:** Regular steam working ends on the main line north of York following intro-duction of more diesels on freight turns but York 9F 2-10-0s and B1 4-6-0s still venture to the East Midlands.

**August, 1966:** The first Brush Type 4 (Class 47) diesels in the D1100 series (D1100/1) are delivered new to York depot.

**1.9.66:** The last active V2 in England, York's 60831, called to take over the 17.00 Newcastle-Liverpool from failed Type 4 diesel D395 at Durham while returning to York after delivering a freight to Tyne Yard.

**Above: At one side of the roundhouse stood a small covered area of straight tracks which formed an entrance to part of the repair shop. Present on 14th January, 1963 was Newton Heath Black Five No.44893.**

Ex-LNWR 0-8-0s were among many foreign engines working to York and as Bert Lodge, an engineman at Mirfield, West Yorkshire, relates, they were far from welcome:

"My first sight of York was as a fireman working the 4.10pm Holyhead-York train of Irish cattle. It ran seven days a week and was often powered by a 'Wessy D'.

"We usually terminated in York Yard South except on market days when, if the cattle were for auction, we took them straight to Foss Islands. From there we went to the shed for coal and water before returning home light engine.

"There wouldn't be a soul in sight as we approached the outside foreman's office until they heard our hissing, groaning fog machine. Then they were out like rats from a sinking ship.

"Don't leave that here. You're only here for coal and water. We don't want the b*!*! thing," they'd shout.

"You could see the relief on their faces when we told them we were going home light engine after getting coal, water and a drink of tea. A 'Wessy D' put the Fear of God into York men.

"And no wonder, anyone trying to move a 'D' without knowing exactly what he was doing was asking for trouble as it was apt to use the shed wall as a buffer stop."

**Above: The strange sight in the repair shop on 27th November, 1965 was ex-LMS 3F 0-6-0T No.47564 minus cab, bunker and side tanks but in excellant external condition and carrying the number 2022. The locomotive had been converted, presumably at Darlington works, for use as a stationary boiler on the London Midland Region, and was in the repair shop for attention while en route back across the Pennines.** (Brian Myland)

**Below: Inside the repair shop on 26th September, 1965 was J27 No.65894.** (Keith Preston)

Above: This grimy but glorious spectacle was the view across York MPD yards on 8th June, 1963. A paradise for spotters but the air was always thick with smoke not enjoyed by residents on the other side of the river. V2 No.60864 and B1 No.61198 coming off shed together demonstrate how busy York was in those days.

Centre: Entertainment for enthusiasts touring the depot on 4th October, 1964 after arriving on a railtour hauled by Britannia No.70020 *Mercury*, was provided by K1 No.62049 when it derailed outside the roundhouse. (*Keith Preston*)

Bottom: By the house in the background, at the end of North Eastern Crescent, was one place where spotters gained illicit access to the shed yard. Worth noting on 20th June, 1959 was ex-Great Central A5 4-6-2T No.69803, posed alongside K3 No.61899. (*Brian Myland*)

Above: Malton J27 No.65888 proudly displays its 50F shedplate while stabled in yard on 14th January, 1963. A couple of months later Malton shed was closed and it became a York engine. Behind the locos are the diesel fuel tanks(still there in 1994) and the inexplicable fixed distant signal protecting the siding.

Centre: A manual coal stage stood near this spot until the 1930s when the mechanical coaling plant was built. Loaded wagons were shunted up the concrete ramp into the timber shed, emptied and the coal tipped into engine tenders by hand. The NER Atlantic being replenished was LNER Class C7 No.2206. *(Cecil Ord)*

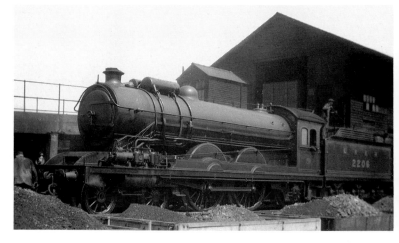

Bottom: Regular York shed pilot until the mid-1950s was this diminutive T.W. Worsdell Y8 0-4-0T. LNER No.8091, seen here in the early 1950s, never carried its BR number. *(Ernest Sanderson)*

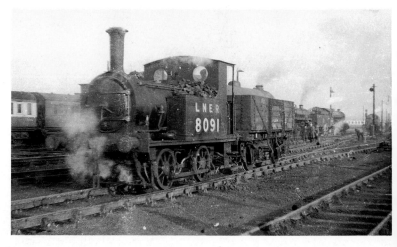

Top: D8312 was one of a batch of new Class 20 diesels which ousted York's last steam locos from trip freights and engineers trains. The victor stands alongside the vanquished B1s and K1s in May, 1967.

Centre: NER 0-8-0s were infrequent visitors in the 1960s and when Q6 No.63450 reached the depot on 9th August, 1967, it was only on its way to the scrapyard.

Bottom: Steam facilities were still intact at York shed in September, 1968 when preserved GWR 4-6-0 No.7029 *Clun Castle* was having its smokebox cleaned over the ash pits after arriving with a railtour. This was believed to be the first visit by a large GWR engine and Eastern Region civil engineers spent several weeks checking clearances along its route to make sure that its wider cylinders would clear platforms and other lineside fixtures. As a result, *Clun Castle* was banned from using platforms 8 or 9 at the station. *(All Stephen Chapman)*

Above: This was the kind of motive power variety which could be found at York during the heyday of steam. Saltley Royal Scot No.46160 *Queen Victoria's Rifleman*, in superb condition, keeps company with A4 No.60006 *Sir Ralph Wedgewood* while being prepared for the 12.43 Newcastle-Bristol on 14th March, 1962. The A4 is not the original *Sir Ralph* which was destroyed during the 1942 air raid, but a renamed engine previously called *Gadwall*.

Below: Pioneer V2 No.60800 *Green Arrow*, visiting York on 9th April, 1962, was the first of 184 V2s and was built in 1936 to haul the Green Arrow express goods service. The class turned out to be very capable on all kinds of work, express passenger included, and their feats of haulage during the second world war became legendary. In 1994 No.60800 could still be seen at the National Railway Museum, in its original form as LNER No.4771.

Visiting tanks on York shed:
Right: Scarborough's BR Standard Class 3 2-6-2T No.82026 awaits its return to the seaside on 1st September, 1962. The loco could have worked in with a midday van train which frequently employed these engines at the time.

Left: Fairburn Class 4 2-6-4T No.42269 was in the process of being transferred from Glasgow Eastfield to the West Riding when it dropped in at York on 15th November, 1964. Clifton carriage sidings, complete with the old 1920s carriage washer, are in the background.
*(Brian Myland)*

Right: V3 2-6-2Ts were not often seen at York even though quite a few were based in the NE Region. No.67677 of Hull Dairycoates was looking in a sorry state on 26th February, 1963 and was probably on its way to Darlington for scrap.

The Robinson-designed 2-8-0s introduced by the Great Central Railway in 1911 routinely worked to York with mineral trains from GC lines in the East Midlands until their demise in 1965.

Top: Many were rebuilt into various forms by the LNER, the final version being the 04/8s with B1 boilers, such as No.63827 of Staveley shed, pictured on 26th February, 1963.

Centre: Fifty eight of the class were modernised with B1 boilers, new cylinders and Walschaert's valve gear and reclassified 01. No.63712 of Tyne Dock shed was untypically clean but minus coupling rods on 7th November, 1962.

Bottom: Many of the GC 2-8-0s were so filthy that it was impossible to make out their cabside numbers. This Class 04/3, one of the batch built for the Railway Operating Division during the first world war, can only be identified as No.63666 because its number is chalked on top of the grime.

Above: New England A3 No.60065 *Knight of Thistle* makes a refreshing sight with its smart paintwork, Great Northern tender and original dome on 1st September, 1962.

Below: A general view of the yard looking from the coaling plant towards the shed with Burton-based Jubilee No.45598 *Basutoland* in company with Mexborough WD 2-8-0 No.90136 on 14th March, 1962. Also present are local B1 No.61198, A4 No.60006 *Sir Ralph Wedgewood* and Royal Scot No.46160 *Queen Victoria's Rifleman*. How many other places could produce an A4 sandwiched between a Jubilee and a Royal Scot?

Above: Snowplough-fitted J27 No.65890 is ready to draw loaded wagons off the bank and on to the coaling plant hoist while acting as depot pilot on 14th March, 1962. Known locally as `Loco Joe,' this task was regularly performed by the J27s after they were replaced by 2-6-0s on local pick-up work.

Below: The driver of Wellingborough 9F 2-10-0 No.92029 finds time for a chat with two young spotters while waiting in the queue for the coaling plant on 1st September, 1962. No.92029 was one of the 9Fs fitted with the Franco-Crosti boiler which had a flue underneath enabling exhaust gases to be used for pre-heating the feedwater, thereby improving thermal efficiency. By the time 92029 was photographed, however, they had all been rebuilt as conventional engines.

The pictures on this page and the next show how locomotives progressed through the facilities at York MPD.

Top: Royal Scot No.46113 *Cameronian* and an A3 have their fires raked out over the ash pit on 29th October, 1962.

Centre: Next port of call was the coaling plant where Britannia No.70020 *Mercury* has its tender refilled after working in with a railtour on 4th October, 1964. *(Keith Preston)*

Bottom: The reinforced concrete coaling plant was commissioned in 1932 as part of a government-sponsored modernisation programme which also included the installation of a 70ft electric turntable. It could hold 500 tons of coal, feed two locomotives at a time, and was demolished, with considerable difficulty, in 1970. A pair of WD 2-8-0s have just been replenished while B1 No.61199 stands in the yard on 13th September, 1966.

Above: After coaling, engines would move on to the 70ft turntable which was at the very top end of the yard. Jubilee No.45620 *North Borneo*, a visitor from Burton-on-Trent, looks impressive while turning there on 30th March, 1962.
Below: On the same day, York B16/2 No.61438, one of those rebuilt by Sir Nigel Gresley from 1937, has come off the turntable and is now taking water.

Top: A4 No.60016 *Silver King* had a full tender and was about to be turned ready to return south on 25th February, 1963.

Centre: The bitterly cold air of that day caused plenty of steam to rise from V2 No.60877 as it moved away from the turntable.

Bottom: On 30th March, 1963, Gateshead-based A4 No.60020 *Guillemot* leaves the coaling plant followed by Jubilee No.45681 *Aboukir* which had just come off the special on page 52. Another Jubilee is on the left while the steam grab used for removing ash from the ash pits beyond the coaling plant is also present.

CLIFTON MOTIVE POWER DEPOT - Enginemen in charge of locomotives en route to the Locomotive Departure Sidings must stop and report to the Outlet Cabin and give details of trains to be worked by the locomotives. Unless otherwise instructed, they must proceed via the Shed Spur Line to the appropriate Locomotive Departure Siding. Locomotives must be brought to a stand clear of the exit from each siding and should not draw forward from the Departure siding unless called forward through the loudspeaker. Instructions will also be given over the loudspeaker, when necessary, to alter the sequence of locomotives on the Locomotive Departure siding. *Eastern Region Northern Area Sectional Appendix, 1968.*

Above: As this view shows, the B16s were handsome engines and it is a tragedy that not one was preserved. B16/2 No.61457 stands near the turntable on 14th March, 1962.
Below: Another classic type lost to preservation was the ex-LMS Patriot 4-6-0. No.45515 *Caernarvon* stands in the yard after turning on 17th March, 1961 while a Royal Scot sits in the background. Clifton carriage sidings form the backdrop. Since the 1970s, most of this area has been covered by industrial units while the carriage depot is now a housing estate.

**Top:** Visiting York shed on 14th May, 1962 was ex-Ministry of Supply J94 0-6-0ST No.68011 of Ardsley shed, probably on its way back home after overhaul at Darlington works.

**Centre:** Doubtless A8 4-6-2T No.69886, photographed on 6th March, 1960, was not in a hurry to complete its journey to Darlington for scrapping. It spent several months at this spot near the turntable but had made it to the scrapyard by June. *(Brian Myland)*

**Bottom:** A non-BR visitor in 1969 was brand new master and slave diesel shunter No. 201, on its way from the Thomas Hill Vanguard works near Rotherham to the British Steel Corporation's Cleveland plant near Middlesbrough. No.201 was the first of five such Vanguard locomotives built in 1969 for the Cleveland works. *(Ernest Sanderson)*

# SHORT MEMORIES

**December, 1966:** York's last V2, 60831, is withdrawn.

**February, 1967:** About a dozen active steam locomotives remain on York's books, mainly B1 4-6-0s and K1 2-6-0s.

**18.3.67:** Nineteen steam locomotives found in York shed on this day include eight B1s, five K1s, Jubilee 45675 *Hardy* used for crew training, and preserved A4 60019 *Bittern*.

**30.5.67:** Jubilee 45562 *Alberta* hauls the Royal Train conveying the Duke of Edinburgh, from York to Ripon and back. The train is brought into York from the south by two Type 2 diesels.

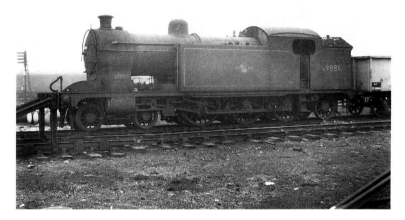

Top: This pre-1923 scene shows NER Class Z(LNER C7) 4-4-2 No.706 getting into its stride past Clifton carriage sidings with a northbound express. Before the Gresley Pacifics came on the scene, the NE Atlantics were regarded as the blue riband power of the East Coast main line. *(Cecil Ord)*

Bottom: Forty years later, Gateshead A4 No.60001 *Sir Ronald Matthews* accelerates past the same spot with the northbound Flying Scotsman on 1st September, 1962 while deputising for a diesel. York Minster dominates the skyline, and the motive power depot is on the right while Black Five No.44734 and Jubilee No.45652 *Hawke* pause in Clifton carriage sidings with the Newcastle-Manchester Red Bank empty news vans.

Centre: Passing the opposite way with an Up express freight on 14th March, 1963 was well-polished V2 No.60908.

Having left Clifton and crossed over Leeman Road, the 1877 main line swings round Severus curve to come alongside the 1841 Darlington route at Severus Junction, also known as Gas Works Junction and finally as York Yard North.

Top: Looking south across York yards from York Yard North on 25th January, 1984. Severus curve is on the left while the 1841 route goes straight ahead, between York Up yard in the centre, the Down yard and carriage works on the right. Much, including the Up Yard hump, is still intact in 1994 but the view is obstructed by the overhead wires of electrification. *(Stephen Chapman)*

Centre: Menial work for one of the illustrious A4s. No.60019 *Bittern* crosses Skelton bridge and the River Ouse with a coke train on 15th April, 1963. Beyond the bridge is Skelton Bridge Junction, the northern extremity of the York complex, and the point where the slow lines diverged left into Skelton New Yard, opened in 1941 and closed in the 1970s.

Bottom: Thumping round Severus curve with a 1960s northbound railtour is preserved A3 *Flying Scotsman*. *(Ernest Sanderson)*

# THE MYSTERIOUS TRIANGLE

In an area north west of the station and sandwiched between the 1841 and 1877 main lines was a complex of marshalling yards, workshops and depots where just about every kind of railway business went on, as it still does in 1994. Well hidden from public view, this fascinating hive of activity could have been called the mysterious triangle.

Above: Cattle vans line up at Holgate cattle docks on 9th May, 1962 as 8F 2-8-0 No.48160 and B16/2 No.61438 emerge from York yards and take the curve round to Holgate Junction with southbound freights.

Below: Another type of 2-8-0 to regularly reach York was the ex-GNR Class 02 based at such places as Doncaster and Grantham. No.63961, heading towards Holgate Junction with a train of petrol tanks on 16th May, 1962, is a Retford engine.

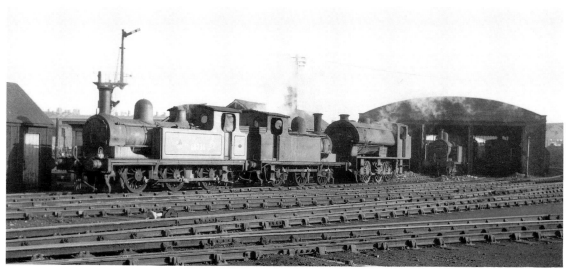

One of the greatest mysteries was what lay behind the public face of the South shed, closed in the 1950s but still used for stabling yard and station pilots until the early 60s.

Top: Celebrity J72 No.68736 was in company with unsung classmate No.68686, J94 0-6-0ST No.68061 and 3F 0-6-0T No.47448 at the north end of the GNE straight shed on 7th February, 1961.

Centre: The working life of Scottish D49/1 4-4-0 No.62702 *Oxfordshire* was over when it was stored on the station side of the straight shed.

Bottom: Engines visiting York and Branches yards still went to South shed for water and stabling, as seen on 10th April, 1962 with K3 2-6-0s 61847(left) and 61969. The surviving 1851 roundhouse is behind 61969 while the roofless 1863 roundhouse is behind 61847.

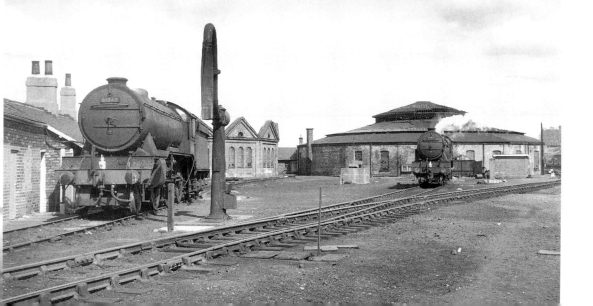

Top: York's ex-Midland Railway 3F 0-6-0T No.47239 (front) and ex-LMS 3F No.47556 stand cold alongside the shed on 17th April, 1961 as B1 No.61030 *Nyala* makes its way into York yards.

The Midland, which from 1879 leased the larger roundhouse from the NER, was among a number of companies with engines based at York. In 1933, its successor, the LMS, took over the straight shed which was coded 19F in the company's Sheffield district. On nationalisation, York South became a sub-shed of 50A.

Centre: The kind of delight which young spotters creeping round the South shed hoped to find - J25 0-6-0 No.65675 stored in the larger roundhouse.

Bottom: Although of NER origin, this roundhouse had a distinctly Midland look about it. WD 2-8-0 No.90663 was stored by the shed entrance on 1st September, 1962 while B1 No.61240 *Harry Hinch-cliffe* and Gresley motive power department coach No.DE320765 were alongside.

# SHORT MEMORIES

**11.7.67:** York depot turns out preserved A4 60019 *Bittern* for duty on a parcels train to Newcastle. The run is repeated the following day.

**2.4.69:** Class 50 diesel 408 arrives at York light engine from Darlington.

**October, 1969:** Prototype 4,000hp Brush diesel *Kestrel* begins regular trial running through York on the 07.55 Kings Cross-Newcastle and 15.45 return.

# SHORT MEMORIES

**22.3.70:** Contractors try to blow up the 100ft high reinforced concrete coaling plant at York North with only partial success. Over the following weeks heavy plant and even locomotives with steel hausers are used in the struggle to break up the seemingly indistructible edifice.

**3.4.72:** Leeman Road goods depot closes.

**16.9.72:** Preserved A4 60019 *Bittern*, now restored as No.19 in post-war LNER blue livery, hauls a 12-coach special from York to Scarborough and back as BR tentatively begins to lift its notorious four-year main line steam ban.

**Top:** There was still life in the officially closed straight shed on 7th February, 1961 as J94 No.68046 took a break from shunting in Branches Yard alongside classmate 68061 and J72 No.69003.

**Centre:** The South shed's small manual coaling stage was still in situ when K1 No.62047 was photographed nearby on 3rd April, 1962. This view is looking towards York Yard South with Branches Yard on the right.

**Bottom:** Class O2 2-8-0 No.63935 passes the yardmaster's office on its way into York yards with a goods from the south on 21st May, 1962. The footbridge carries an alley known as Cinder Path which connects Leeman Road with Holgate Road.

Top: Yet more locomotive variety. This time ex-LMS 0-6-0 No.44098 of Normanton shed leaves York Yard South and passes the old signal box on 3rd February, 1961. The girder bridge linking the wagon works(right) and the carriage works on the left has since been removed.

Centre: Having passed the South shed, ex-LMS 'Crab' 2-6-0 No.42865, also of Normanton, brings a through freight between the York Yard South old and new signal boxes on 1st May, 1962.

Bottom: Viewed from the new box with the Down yard hump in the background, Class 04/8 2-8-0 No.63841 draws up alongside the old box on 1st August, 1962.

## SHORT MEMORIES

**Autumn, 1973:** Sugar beet no longer received by rail at York factory, meaning the end of such traffic from Elvington on the DVLR.

The 1951 resignalling did not include the lines through York yards which remained under the control of local boxes until the solid state system was commissioned in 1989. In 1962, however, the old York Yard South signal box was replaced by the new electric box on the opposite side of the line. On 1st August, 1962, signal and telegraph engineers were dismantling the mechanical lever frame in the old box(top) while(centre) the signalman looks well pleased with his new push-button panel.

Bottom: York wagon works, founded by the NER in 1867 and eventually covering 17 acres, built a variety of goods vehicles and repaired as many as 400 a week. It was closed in 1966 under a BR workshops reshaping programme, though the shop in this view was still in business as a repair depot in 1994. With the works on the left, decidedly crumpled 04/8 No.63781 ambles a mixed goods into the yards on 3rd February, 1961.

# SHORT MEMORIES

**15.1.75:** The 23.15 Kings Cross-Aberdeen, travelling on the Down Main, and the 19.20 Aberdeen-Kings Cross, arriving at platform 9, collide side-on after the northbound train passes a signal at danger. The guard of the southbound train is injured, two of its coaches are derailed, two coaches and the engine of the northbound train are damaged, as is the platform edge.

**1.9.77:** The first 125mph High Speed Train for the East Coast main line, 254001, is handed over to the Eastern Region general manager in a ceremony at York station. Its arrival is greeted by a fanfare from five Royal Scots Dragoon Guards trumpeters positioned on the footbridge.

Above: This view looking north from the old York Yard South signal box is full of interest, not least the signals pulled off for 9F 2-10-0 No.92184 on 1st May, 1962.
Below: Coming south with the wagon works on the right and the Up yard behind it in February, 1961, is B16/2 4-6-0 No.61455 on a train of empty `hyfit' wagons.

**Above:** With the Up yard on the left, 04/1 2-8-0 No.63917, one of the original Robinson GC batch, manoevres a line of wagons out of the Down Yard. This area faces directly north and in winter icy winds sweep through, earning it the nickname `Klondyke Yard.'

**Centre:** On 11th January, 1961, 8F No.48194 was moving a through freight southwards past the Up yard with its regulator open and continuous blowdown in operation, causing steam to come from under the cab.

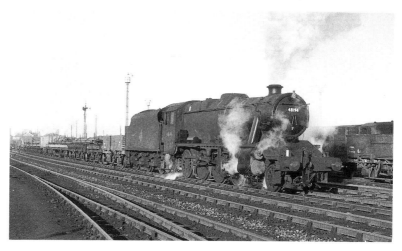

In 1994, the northern half of the Down yard was still used for engineers wagons but the southern end was abandoned in the 1970s. The Up yard was still largely intact, handling coal trains and engineers traffic.

**Bottom:** Looking south over the carriage works in the late 1970s with 350hp diesel shunter No.08062 on pilot duties. York Down yard is on the left while new Class 455 electric trains for the Southern Region are among stock in the works yard.

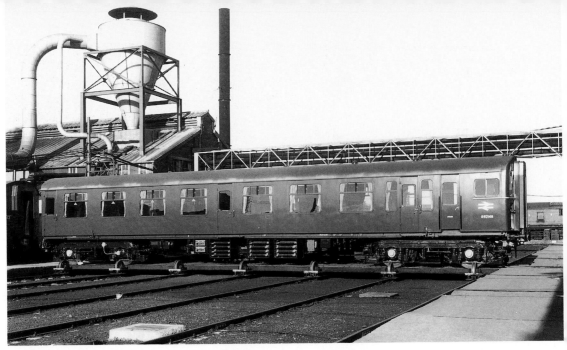

Above: Traversers are a normal feature of large railway workshops and allow vehicles to be moved between tracks without the need for space-consuming point-work. On 23rd February, 1967, the York carriage works traverser was moving a coach from one of the new electric units being built for the Waterloo-Bournemouth line.

Centre: Diesel multiple units were an important part of the workload at York works in 1994. The first prototype Class 150 Sprinters were built there in 1984, followed by the Class 150/2s and, during the 1990s, many Networker Turbo trains for the London area. Older diesel units were also repaired there, such as this Metro-Cammell power car, pictured on 31st January, 1961.

Bottom: Again in common with other major railway work-shops, York had its own fire brigade, pictured here on 7th February 1958. (All by courtesy of British Rail)

**Right:** Contained within the mysterious triangle was Leeman Road goods depot and the yard leading up to it. The warehouse presented a busy scene handling all kinds of freight sundries on 31st January, 1961 but by 1972 it was owned by the road-orientated National Carriers Ltd., BR concentrating its freight activities at Foss Islands. *(By courtesy of British Rail)*

**Centre:** Next to the goods depot was the Central Concrete Depot which manufactured small concrete items for much of British Railways. It is now closed but in 1974 this steam-powered grab was still busy loading sand and gravel into the mixing hopper. *(Stephen Chapman)*

**Bottom:** At the far end of Leeman Road, on the Down side of Severus Curve, was the District Engineer's permanent way yard where, in this 1960s view, a new double line junction was being assembled. *(Ernest Sanderson)*

# SHORT MEMORIES

**Summer, 1978:** Derwent Valley Railway revenue shows a 12.5 per cent increase over 1977 enabling a dividend to be paid to shareholders.

**Autumn, 1981:** Deltic mania grips York as enthusiasts travel from all the country to see the world-famous diesels working out their last weeks on trains to Kings Cross and Liverpool.

**20.9.83:** High Speed Train power car 43064 is named *City of York* by the Lord Mayor, Councillor S.F. Galloway.

Top: Just over a mile from York station, 350hp diesel No.08707 struggles to bring the morning Smarty Express past the NER slotted signal guarding the exit from the Foss islands branch onto the Scarborough line at Burton Lane Junction. It was 11th January, 1984 and the 08 was slipping constantly while trying to move its huge load of air-braked vans away to Dring-houses yard. *(Stephen Chapman)*

## ACROSS THE OUSE

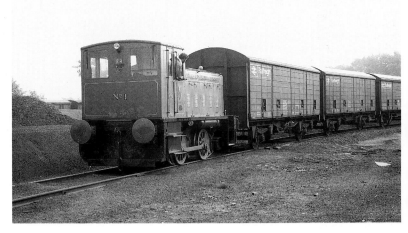

Right: The Foss Islands branch served a number of industrial concerns, the biggest being Rowntree's chocolate factory which had an extensive rail system operated by five steam 0-4-0STs until they were replaced by diesels in 1958. Rowntree-Mackintosh No.1(Ruston 423661 built in 1958) was one of four diesels there on 20th June, 1979 when it was dealing with air-braked vans in the factory yard. *(Adrian J.Booth)*

FOSS ISLANDS BRANCH: The regulations for Working Single Lines of Railway by Train Staff and Ticket apply between a point opposite Burton Lane Down Branch Starting signal and Foss Islands goods station, with the following modification:-

The Staff and Tickets are in the charge of the signalman at Burton Lane and, between 07.30 and 16.30, the Staff Attendant at Foss Islands. Between 16.30 and 07.30, no person is in charge at Foss Islands and during this period only one train must be on the single line at one time. The driver of such a train must be in possession of the Train Staff.

When two or more freight trains are required to follow each other on to the branch before 07.30, arrangements must be made by the York Yardmaster for the Staff Attendant at Foss Islands to be in attendance.

When no one is on duty at Foss Islands to receive the Train Staff from the driver, it must be retained for the return journey.

When the driver of a train about to enter the single line at either the Burton Lane or Foss Islands end is given a Ticket numbered 2, 3, 4, 5 or 6, the signalman at Burton Lane, or Staff Attendant at Foss Islands, must inform the driver what interval has elapsed since the departure of the preceeding train. The driver must then proceed at caution, being prepared to stop short of any obstruction. The same practice must be followed in the case of a train carrying the Train Staff when a train has preceeded it with a Ticket.

On arrival of a train at Burton Lane Up Inner Home signal the guard must, if the rear vehicle is clear inside the fouling point, so advise the driver, and the latter must instruct his fireman to hand the Train Staff or Ticket to the Burton Lane signalman, who may, if the train has brought the Train Staff, allow a Down train to leave for Foss Islands...*Eastern Region Northern Area Sectional Appendix, 1968.*

Above Foss Islands was still handling respectable amounts of freight when 350hp diesel No.08771 was placing wagons in the Derwent Valley's Layerthorpe yard on 1st November, 1979. The depot closed in 1986, leaving only spasmodic oil trains to the DVR until the whole branch closed in 1988.

Above right: This slotted signal protected the entrance to Foss Islands. Normally in the `off' position, it went to danger when the points were set for the Derwent Valley.

Right: York power station used two overhead electric engines. One, built by Kerr Stuart in 1912, is preserved at the East Anglian Railway Museum, Chappel and Wakes Colne, Essex, and is seen there in 1979. *(All Stephen Chapman)*

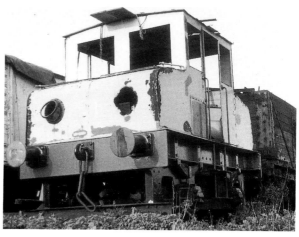

# FOSS ISLANDS c1922

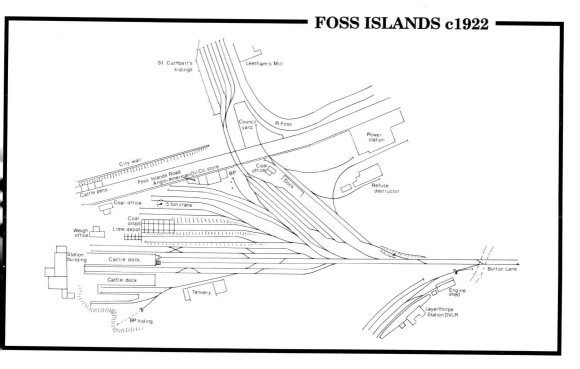

Right: For most of its existance, the Derwent Valley Light Railway hired its locomotives from big brother on the main line. On 8th August, 1967 Drewery 0-6-0 diesel No.D2262 was waiting to leave Layerthorpe with the daily train. Since 1965, this ran as far as Wheldrake but on this particular day the only traffic was a Presflo cement wagon for the concrete works at Osbaldwick.

In 1969, the DVLR purchased Nos.D2298 and D2245 from BR, repainted them in its own grey livery and renumbered them 1 and 2 respectively. D2298 was later repainted green and named *Lord Wenlock*, after the company's first chairman. *(Stephen Chapman)*

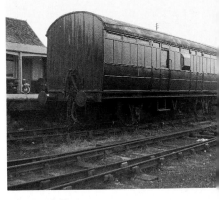

Above right: At the back of the train was ex-BR pigeon brake No.70250.

Above left: In summer, 1977 the DVR introduced a Tuesday-Friday steam passenger service for tourists and bought preserved J72 No.69023 *JoEm* along with a rake of BR coaches which it repainted into its original dark blue and cream livery. Though moderately successful, the venture offered little scope for development and was withdrawn at the end of the 1979 summer season. This special last steam train, waiting to leave Layerthorpe station, was run on 25th November, 1979. *(Both Stephen Chapman)*

Left: The 1947-vintage Fowler 0-4-0 diesel shunter *Churchill* shunted the Highlight Grain Handling depot at Dunnington. It is seen outside the DVR's Layerthorpe engine shed on 27th September, 1981, the day the DVR closed. Inside the shed is another Fowler, DVR 0-4-0 No.4210142. *(Stephen Chapman)*

**Right:** Dunnington, just over 4 miles from Layerthorpe, and *JoEm* rests at the buffers which marked the end of the line on 14th May, 1977. Before 1973, the DVR continued across the main York-Hull road to Elvington and until 1968 to Wheldrake. Before 1965, it ran through to Cliff Common where it joined the Selby-Market Weighton line. *(Stephen Chapman)*

In 1981 the DVR Board concluded that there was more profit in property than railways and closed the line to Dunnington. The last train, seen approaching Layerthorpe on 27th September(below), was a special chartered by the BR Staff Railway Society using *Lord Wenlock* and hired BR coaches. *(Peter Sutch)*

**Above:** The week before, this Gloucester Class 100 DMU, used by BR as an inspection saloon, was loaned to the DVR directors for a farewell run. It is seen between Osbaldwick and Murton on 24th September. *(Both Stephen Chapman)*

**Above:** Making a spectacular start from Layerthorpe on 13th April, 1977 with one of several special trains it worked through to the DVR is the National Railway Museum's LNWR 2-4-0 No.790 *Hardwicke*. In 1993, this section of the DVR and all the Foss Islands branch were converted into a footpath and cycle track. *(Stephen Chapman)*

The railway around York changed dramatically between 1969 and 1989 when depots and yards closed, local freight ended and the whole area was rationalised and resignalled for the East Coast electrification. These few pages are dedicated to scenes from the 1970s and 80s which have themselves become history.

Right: In their final years, the Deltics, ousted from top link duty by High Speed Trains, were allocated to York depot and used mainly on semi-fast trains to Kings Cross. On Saturday 27th June, 1981, No.55016 *Gordon Highlander* was on an Edinburgh to Kings Cross relief. Since then, this track layout has been slimmed down and the sidings on the extreme right turned into a car park.

Below: In the early 1980s, Class 123 Inter-City DMUs from the Western Region were transferred to Hull for use on some Trans-Pennine services, including those between Hull, Leeds and Morecambe. The 11.17 to Leeds was waiting at platform 11 with car No.E52095 leading on 25th July, 1982. (*Both Stephen Chapman*)

# CHANGE AT YORK

**Right:** On Sunday 25th June, 1978, British Rail's first steam service for ten years ran from York to Leeds, Harrogate and back to York. The very first train was the 09.55 departure hauled by preserved V2 No.4771 *Green Arrow*, seen waiting to leave platform 9. In Queen Street sidings on the right, are car carriers used on the Motorail car sleeper service to Inverness. *(Stephen Chapman)*

**Bottom:** In the 1980s, the steam service ran to Scarborough and ex-LMS Pacific No.46229 *Duchess of Hamilton* was about to leave platform 7 with the Scarborough Spa Express on 16th June, 1983. The bay platforms are full of coaches but after the 1988/89 remodelling only platform 7 and the siding next to it remained, while platforms 4-6 became a car park. *(by courtesy of British Rail)*

**Centre:** Recalling the 1960s when a Pacific was regularly kept on stand-by in case of diesel failures - only it was preserved A4 No.60009 *Union of South Africa* on 13th August, 1984. By then steam was so routine at York that a new servicing point, complete with inspection pit, was set up on the site of Queen Street shed.

The North shed repair shop became the diesel depot but lost its main line allocation at the end of 1981. It carried out light servicing on visiting locomotives for another year before being sold to the National Railway Museum. York retained a small number of Class 08 diesel shunters but, used mainly by the engineer's department, they were re-allocated to the wagon depot and refuelled at the civil engineer's plant workshops, sharing modified facilities with track maintenance machines.

Top: Class 20s Nos.20013, 20244 and 20162 line up at the north end of the loco yard on 13th February, 1985. On the right is the new Clifton carriage shed, built with a European grant in 1982. This modern depot lasted barely five years before being made redundant by the replacement of loco-hauled Trans-Pennine expresses with Sprinters maintained at Leeds. No other use could be found for it and the whole depot was demolished.

Centre: The English Electric Class 40s were the first main line diesels allocated to York which had as many as 30 at any one time. No.251 stands outside the roundhouse in June, 1972, on what is now the NRM's outdoor display area. (Stephen Chapman)

Bottom: Looking into the repair shop in 1975 when preserved GNR Atlantic No.990 Henry Oakley was steamed for the first time in over 20 years. (Ernest Sanderson)

**Above: The last green-liveried Class 40 No.40106 hauls a southbound mixed goods out of York yards on 29th May, 1980. Wagonload freight such as this was on its way out, one of the reasons why the Down yard hump was abandoned in the 1970s.** *(Stephen Chapman)*

**Below: In June, 1977, British Rail marked the centenary of york station with a weekend exhibition in platforms 4-6. A number of engines from the National Railway Museum were put on show, including Tennant 2-4-0 No.910 which was already two years old when the station was opened. Other exhibits included Class M1 4-4-0 No.1621, GNR 4-2-2 No.1, LNWR 2-4-0 No.790 *Hardwicke* and A4 No.4468 *Mallard*, plus a number diesel locomotives and freight wagons.** *(Stephen Chapman)*

One of York's busiest days in modern times was 31st August, 1982 when 87 extra trains arrived for the visit of Pope John Paul 11, a similar number of departures taking the pilgrims home again.

Thirty two were loco-hauled from the North East, West and South Yorkshire, Hull, Scarborough and even one from Norwich. The rest were diesel multiple units or High Speed Trains.

Trains began arriving in the early hours and once their passengers had disembarked were sent off again to collect more pilgrims. To avoid running round, trains from the North East went to Sheffield or Huddersfield, for example, and those arriving from South Yorkshire to the North East.

Accommodating the empty stock until the return departures was itself a major exercise. Eight trains were stabled at Clifton carriage sidings, two on Clifton Up Goods line, one on the carriage washer line, three in Holgate Down sidings, eight in Dringhouses yard, two in Queen Street sidings, two in the Fruit Dock sidings, one in the old platform one, one each in platforms 5 and 15, and one on the engine line between 14 and 15. Two sets went to Malton.

The station also had to cope with all the usual traffic on the busiest Bank Holiday of the year.

Top: The prototype High Speed Train ran trials between York and Darlington in the early 1970s when it set a new world speed record for diesel traction of 143.2 mph. Later in the 1970s, the HST's Class 41 power cars were back in action, this time taking electric power car No.SC49003 from the ill-fated Advanced Passenger Train for high speed tests, seen passing through the station on 15th September, 1978.

Centre: Even this view can no longer be seen. A Class 141 railbus in West Yorkshire PTE green and cream livery arrives from Harrogate at platform 12 as a Metro-Cammell DMU prepares to leave platform 13. The 141s are now in red and cream, DMUs are no longer seen at York and the track has been removed from platform 12.

Bottom: The moment when the view of York station seen in many earlier pages of this book changed for good. On 23rd October, 1988 a pair of 12 tonne cranes undertook remodelling work which resulted in removal of the centre tracks between platforms 8 and 9. (Stephen Chapman)

# SHORT MEMORIES

8.11.84: York-based 350hp diesel shunter 08525 is named *Percy the Pilot* by transport minister David Mitchell after he opens the new travel centre and refurbished concourse.

1.11.87: An InterCity 125 breaks the world speed record for diesel traction when it achieves 148 mph north of York.